THE BUSY MOM'S
GUIDE TO SIMPLE LIVING

THE BUSY MOM'S
GUIDE TO SIMPLE LIVING

Creative Ideas and Practical Ways
For Making The Most Out of What You Have

JACKIE WELLWOOD

CROSSWAY BOOKS • WHEATON, ILLINOIS
A DIVISION OF GOOD NEWS PUBLISHERS

The Busy Mom's Guide to Simple Living

Copyright © 1997 by Jackie Wellwood

Published by Crossway Books
    a division of Good News Publishers
    1300 Crescent Street
    Wheaton, Illinois 60187.

Cover Design: Cindy Kiple

Printed in the United States of America

ISBN1-56865-485-5

Table of Contents

Acknowledgments

A BOOK OF THIS NATURE HAPPENS ONLY BY THE GRACE OF GOD. The many hours I spent working on "our" book were backed up by many hours of support from my loving family. I could not have written the book without them, and at times I was not sure I could complete it with them. And so it goes in the life of a mother.

To Jim, my loving husband. I thank you for your tireless efforts at trying to run the household while I was writing. I'm sorry that our styles of organizing are so different and that it was hard for you to do it "my way." Thank you for the character-building experience of having to sort through all that you decided to do "your way." Another book or two and I believe we could learn to work together like a well-oiled machine. You did a fine job!

To Jamie, my oldest daughter. What a blessing it is that you learned how to cook entire meals from scratch. Your homemade bread is excellent!

To Jenny, my look-alike, who always brought me a cup of tea at just the right time. Your diligence is much appreciated.

To Jimmy, my oldest son, a young man with great patience when I could not spend as much time reading to him as he wanted. Thank you for waiting. I'm back.

To Jonathan, my hard worker, who has learned how to serve others at a very young age. I thank you for your efforts.

To Joanna, my smiling two-year-old. What a joy it is to be surrounded by your enthusiasm. Yes, Mommy can play now.

To Josiah, my darling son, who spent my writing time in utero. Welcome to our big, happy family!

And to all of the many others who offered encouragement, I extend my gratitude for the role that each one of you played in this work.

To God be the glory!

Preface

GOOD HOMEMAKING SKILLS DON'T JUST HAPPEN. THEY ARE learned—most often on the job. As busy moms we need instruction to facilitate a successful blending of the many responsibilities that make up our days. Even if classes were available to us, it is doubtful that very many of us could spend enough time learning what we need to know. It is for these reasons that I present this homemaking handbook to you as an opportunity to cover a wide range of topics in a relatively short amount of time.

I have been a mom for ten years. In that time I have been blessed with six precious children. I have had to make many decisions, fill many roles at one time, learn a myriad of new skills, and have been more tired than I ever thought possible. My fatigue forced me to seek a healthier lifestyle, which led to drastic changes in the way we eat. I cook from scratch and buy much of our food in bulk. We also can and freeze fruits and vegetables. Our single income requires more creative approaches to saving money. Gifts that we give now come from the heart instead of the department store. As our family grows we have found it essential to be organized in the areas of chores, cleaning, and laundry. I have read countless how-to books that left me feeling hopelessly behind in my work. Although these books presented practical helps, they didn't assist me in deciding which ideas to use and which ones to ignore.

This book is a combination of practical skills *and* decision-making philosophy. Rather than encouraging you to "do it all," I will help you answer the question, "What should I do now?" The answers will vary depending upon the unique needs of your own family. This book is a resource to help you integrate the many facets of your role into a workable routine that is satisfying instead of stifling.

As I work out my own routines in my home, I realize that the decision-making process I use is much different than the way I worked as a child or in college. Five years after I was married, a well-known verse in the book of John took on new meaning for me: "For God so loved the world that he gave his one and only Son, that whoever believes in him shall not perish but have eternal life" (John 3:16). I learned that I needed to take action regarding my sin and ask God to forgive me. It was Christ who died for my sins, and I needed to have a relationship with Him. "I am the way and the truth and the life. No one comes to the Father except through me," He tells us (John 14:6). My understanding of the Bible and how God works in my life is a daily growing process. The Bible is now my source of direction and guides me as I try to keep my household in order.

With a new focus of pleasing the Lord instead of pleasing myself, I find that I make my decisions differently than I did before I became a Christian. In 2 Corinthians 5:15 we read, "And he died for all, that those who live should no longer live for themselves but for him who died for them and was raised again." You will find throughout this book that many of my choices run counter to our culture. This is true in part because in walking with Jesus I am choosing not to follow the world's order for things. "Do not love the world or anything in the world. If anyone loves the world, the love of the Father is not in him. For everything in the world—the cravings of sinful man, the lust of his eyes and the boasting of what he has and does—comes not from the Father but from the world. The world and its desires pass away, but the man who does the will of God lives forever" (1 John 2:15-17).

I have arranged this book so that you do not need to read it cover to cover unless that is your desire. Each chapter stands alone and can be referred to as your interests dictate. I advise you to change slowly as too much too quickly can easily overwhelm and discourage you. I have found this out by experience. It will be most encouraging to read a little and then implement what you have learned. The satisfaction that comes will spur you on to the next area that you wish to explore.

The topics covered in this book are in no way exhaustive. I would rather that you be successful at beginning with a few basics than be overwhelmed with too many choices. Each chapter has a detailed resource section (toward the end of the book) to help you locate more specialized materials on that particular topic should you desire further information.

I have not always been a homemaker. My training in college prepared me for work in business; I worked as a mortgage loan officer. I have a B.S. degree in Business with a specialization in Management. I assumed that my training in management would provide me with all I would need to manage my home. This was not at all the case. Two business principles actually hindered me as a mom.

The first is the concept of productivity. At first glance, it seemed that all would be well to be a "productive" mom. But if we define productivity as how much we get done (which can be measured quantitatively), we will miss out on many of the joys of motherhood. If we are spending more time cleaning than playing with our children, we may be out of balance in our role as mothers. Though we do have the responsibility of cleaning and organizing our home, it should not take most of our waking hours.

The second principle is the concept of downtime. In the business world this term refers to non-productive time. In a factory it may mean that the machinery is broken. In an office it may mean that the computer is down. In the home, downtime is a God-given blessing. Each and every day we should have some quiet, unstructured time that does not require us to accomplish any particular task. Time to rest is good.

As a new mom I tried to apply the concepts of productivity and downtime to my home in the same manner I'd applied them in the office. When my baby was napping, I accelerated my pace to accomplish everything possible during this uninterrupted time. It did not occur to me that when my baby was resting, I should rest as well. Our bodies need to rest, and it would not benefit my family if I neglected this fact. I have sometimes pushed myself too hard to accomplish tasks when I should have been resting. Resting, in my opinion, was just downtime—wasted time.

It did not take long for me to see that my training was inadequate for my job as a mom. Homemaking classes did not fit into the college preparatory track in my high school. I had only one cooking class in college. During our first year of marriage I tried to make yeast bread. I kneaded the bread by hand and followed the recipe, expecting the best. To my surprise I found that when the bread was finished baking, it was only about one and a half inches high. Furthermore, it was very dense and tasted awful. My caring husband would not let me throw it out and graciously ate the entire loaf. It took nine years before I made homemade bread again, and I have been doing it ever since.

It is not easy to try new things. It is even more difficult to try new things when you have a baby crying to be fed or a toddler underfoot trying to help. I hope that throughout this book as I share my own struggles, you will be motivated to keep going. As moms we all juggle many responsibilities. We are referees, comforters, nurturers, cooks, seamstresses, and much more. Working outside the home or home schooling your children adds even more roles into each day. We do many of these things simultaneously, and I desire to encourage you in practical ways that will allow you to fulfill these many responsibilities.

1

Lifestyle Simplification

HAVE YOU EVER WONDERED WHAT IT REALLY MEANS TO LIVE simply? Does it mean to work less or to work more? Does it mean that I only buy the least expensive item that will meet my needs? Does it mean that I need to reevaluate my needs to see if they are even legitimate? How will I even know where to begin the process of lifestyle simplification in my life?

It can be overwhelming to realize that our lifestyles need a major overhaul. It is humbling to conclude that some of our stress-filled busyness is just not necessary. It may be painful to find that we no longer "click" with our friends who are still on the fast track. It is alarming to discover that even though we are armed with our convictions to live more simply, we don't know how. Worse yet, we don't even know where to look to find out what to do. We can't think of anyone we know who lives simply.

My husband and I have asked these questions and experienced these emotions ourselves. The school of hard knocks has been our training ground and continues to be the source of much of our practical application (and inspiration). We did, however, take an opportunity in the spring of 1993 to spend an entire week with a family who lives very simply. They offer a variety of courses in homesteading. Homesteading is an interest for our family because in order to consider moving from the Chicago suburbs to a more rural setting we need to know more about how to "live off the land." While we are now somewhat prepared to do just that, our greatest benefit from our week with the Fahey family was the practical approach to simplifying our own homesteading experience in the suburbs.

I had learned of the Christian homesteading movement in a magazine and suggested that we take one of the Faheys' classes during our vacation.[1] My husband was eager to do this as well, and we began our preparations. I focused my thoughts on the material that would be presented. I desired to learn more about herbs, food storage for winter, organic gardening, cooking, and more. Many other topics intrigued my husband also, so we both left on our trip with great expectations.

We were given some instructions about what to bring. We would be sleeping in a tent and cooking over an open fire. We would be carrying our supplies since we could not drive our van all the way to where we would be staying. This sounded exciting to me, and I felt prepared as we left on our journey with our four children, ranging in age from six months to seven years old. There were some questions in my mind about the facilities, but I was too enthused about the topics to really be concerned. In our search to find an alternative to the fast-paced American lifestyle, we were hard pressed to find people who could teach us what we needed to know. At last we were on our way to be trained by just such a family, and I decided that whatever the circumstances of our stay on the homestead, I would do just fine.

My first character-building experience came shortly after arriving on a beautiful day in a rural area of New York. They had been experiencing a lot of rain there, and since the road that led up a hill near their homestead was not passable in our van, we had to walk quite a bit further than anticipated. I carried our six-month-old on my back while my husband, Jim, encouraged the two- and four-year-olds to keep walking. My seven-year-old's enthusiasm was noticeably waning about halfway up the hill. She and I stopped for a rest, and somehow I already knew this trip was not going to be an easy one.

It was good to learn this early on because I have not found simple living to be easy either. My struggles to live simply are affirmed by a comment that Doris Janzen Longacre makes in her book *Living More with Less*: "The trouble with simple living is that, though it can be joyful, rich, and creative, it isn't simple. Less of what? For more of what? And for whom? Every day the average tradesperson or homekeeper makes a hundred small decisions which, if you stop to think about what causes what, become maddeningly complex."[2] Somehow I had equated the words *simple* and *easy* in my mind. The first moments of my homestead experience gave me a glimpse of the physical demands of simple living. Packing for the trip had introduced me to how many decisions have to be made for such an endeavor. It takes more effort to figure out what kind of food to bring when you are cooking it over an open fire, carrying it up a hill on your back, and have no way to refrigerate it. There are many adjectives to describe simple living, but *easy* is not one of them.

It was refreshing to reach the top of the hill and view the beautiful homestead. I knew it was worth the struggle up the hill with the children to enter such a beautiful place. It is that way with simple living. So often we must work very hard to do what has to be done, but when we are finished we experience much joy at the accomplishment. Eating healthy foods takes more time and effort to prepare it. We may even decide to grow it ourselves. Saving money often means doing something ourselves rather than paying someone else. But when the pace of our life slows down, we have more time to do these things, and a new way of living emerges.

I soon had another opportunity for character building at the homestead. When we were shown where to set up our tents, I needed to use the restroom and asked one of the sons where I would find the outhouse (a simple homestead of the type we were visiting certainly would not have a bathroom with running water). He pointed over to the ground and explained that this was where we would dig our latrine. I could hardly believe my ears. In all of my enthusiasm about the topics that were being taught, I did not even consider the possibility of no outhouse. Before my thoughts could turn to concerns such as toilet paper, my husband pulled out a roll from the backpack. To shorten a rather shocking experience for me, let it suffice to say that I was the first person in our family to use the "facilities," and after a day or two I did not even think about it. We did not have the use of a toilet as we know it, and that was that. I was surprised at how well I could do without something I considered "standard" to my lifestyle. All throughout the week as we were attending classes, I had the opportunity to evaluate aspects of our lifestyle that I could do without or simplify. (We do have two bathrooms!) Although I do not anticipate making changes that would make my life just like the Fahey family, I have made many changes that were inspired by our visit to their homestead.

Many of these changes were made in the first year after we took their class. Now it is a few years later, and the changes are coming more slowly. In part I believe the cultural influences that we have in an urban area make it difficult to live simply. Our educational backgrounds and our training can further complicate the process of lifestyle simplification. I believe further examination of the way we approach our lifestyle will help us understand what we need to change and how we should go about the process.

Living simply is a choice. In a culture of excess it will not just happen. Conscious effort must be made to evaluate what we are doing and why we are doing it. How much time we spend on something must be considered as we feel that time is always running short. If we are not directed in our journey to a more simple life, we risk our lifestyle being nothing more than an exercise in futility; at the end of our hard work we will be no more satisfied than before.

To keep our focus, key Scripture verses encourage us as we continue to make radical lifestyle changes. "Set your minds on things above, not on earthly things" (Colossians 3:2). We live in a time in history when the earthly comforts we enjoy are in great abundance. Just in the two short decades since I graduated from high school, we have seen a dramatic surge in goods that are available to us. I am stunned by the technological advances being made. I appreciate my computer, but I have a hard time understanding that models are becoming obsolete as quickly as six months after they go on the market. Cellular phones are now so popular that I wonder if face-to-face communication will cease to exist in the coming years. While technology has certainly given us many good things, I wonder how many problems are being created in the name of progress. I know that we are already experiencing automated receptionists that answer your telephone call with recordings and offer you options of listening to other recordings and finally give you someone's voice mail, making it difficult or even impossible to talk to a live human being. Who knows if your message was ever received or will be returned? I know that I do not have time to keep calling back only to be directed to voice mail yet one more time.

By setting our minds on things above rather than on earthly things, it is easier for us to say no to these new gadgets that keep coming our way. We can focus on what God would have us do instead of the advertisers who skillfully advise us of our next "need." Dr. Richard Swenson writes, "Today we must begin valuing the things God values and cease valuing those things of no value to Him."[3] We must carefully select only those items that will truly benefit our service to the Lord. Each family must decide for themselves which goods and services are appropriate to their situation. Setting our minds on heaven will greatly limit our choices.

I have already indicated that the simple life is one of hard work. It may be difficult to understand why we would want to work harder in an age that supplies a multitude of labor-saving devices. This complex question becomes easier to understand in light of Colossians 3:23-34: "Whatever you do, work at it with all your heart, as working for the Lord, not for men, since you know that you will receive an inheritance from the Lord as a reward. It is the Lord Christ you are serving." Our work for the Lord is of eternal significance. If we are working long hours to earn more money to buy more things, we are sacrificing our relationships. We reduce our marriages to the status of "ships passing in the night." Our children do not know us. Our church cannot depend on us.

Tim Kimmel comments in *Little House on the Freeway*, "The fact is, we were designed to find completion in relationships—not in material possessions."[4] When we realize that it is the Lord Christ we are serving, we can reevaluate what we are doing and why we are doing it. As we shelve our consumer mind-set, we can consider new opportunities. We may bring Mom home from full-time employment to raise and train her children. We may entertain a career change for Dad that involves a cut in pay but allows him to be home with his family for more hours each week. We may even decide to educate our children at home.

Our family has made all of these decisions. None of them were easy. All of them required sacrifice and rearrangement of our lifestyle. I will also add that they were not made all at once. Lifestyle simplification is a process that should be implemented at as slow a pace as possible for all family members to be able to cope. Sometimes in our enthusiasm we try to change too much too fast and wind up disappointed and demotivated. This has happened to me more than once as Jim boldly implemented the next change in our life before I was ready. It is important to consider all of your family in areas of major change. Most certainly there will be some disgruntled faces for a period of adjustment.

This was true for me when my husband began to turn down our thermostat at night. Since I would be getting up in the middle of the night to nurse the baby, I would experience the crispness of the cool air in our home. I fought the concept for a time until I realized that I just needed to wear heavier pajamas to bed. I am the only one in our large family who had trouble in this area. All of the children were just fine. This winter will be a true test of my adaptability since we have installed a wood-burning stove and will primarily be heating our home with wood instead of with our furnace.

Before you dismiss this idea as too extreme to consider, let me share how we came to this arrangement. In 1985 I gave no thought at all to the cost of heating a home. Both my husband and I worked, and we did not have any children. Since then, through a series of major life decisions I have left my employment as a mortgage loan officer, Jim has left the field of mechanical engineering and became a full-time firefighter, and we have been blessed with six children. I home school our children, Jim is home more and has a steady job, and we have much less money at our disposal than we did over a decade ago. While all of these decisions have been good ones, we have been forced to look for lower-cost alternatives to much of what we need. Sixteen principles help illustrate how the Lord has enabled us to thrive in these circumstances.

Principle #1: *Live Below Your Means*

We purchased our first home in 1985 in a quiet suburb west of Chicago. We were both working at the time and could have afforded a larger home. Instead we bought a two-bedroom home with one bathroom and a two-car garage. The home had only 940 square feet, but we intended to live there for only five years before upgrading. Neither my husband or myself were Christians at the time and did not have the benefit of understanding biblical guidelines for our actions. We were living for ourselves and following the standard the world set before us. This home was only intended as a stepping-stone to a much larger one in the future. In an interesting way, we found this was not God's plan for our family.

Our first child was born in 1986, and because we had purchased a home below what we could afford, I was able to come home full-time to raise our daughter. By 1987 two major changes were made. Most importantly, my husband and I learned of our need for Jesus Christ as our Lord and Savior. With the Bible as our guide, we began to change the way we viewed just about everything. The value we had previously placed on money began to diminish. It was a good thing because about this time my husband lost his job as a mechanical engineer. He had not enjoyed working in this field and desired to change careers anyway.

A job as a firefighter would not pay much to start. It took until August 1988 for him to complete the testing process and be hired on a full-time basis. During the interim months we lived on a fraction of the income both of us had previously been making. Just before Jim lost his job, we refinanced our home and set up an arrangement where we would pay our own property taxes. Taxes are paid in lump sum twice a year in the summer. Construction work was available in the summer, and we were always able to pay on time. By not having money collected monthly in our mortgage payment for taxes, we had a lower monthly cash outlay during the lean winter months when construction workers are laid off.

Our smaller home allowed us to experience these changes without the catastrophic results that come from being stretched financially. We used this home differently than we had planned as well. We lived there for nine and a half years and moved to a slightly larger home just ten weeks before the birth of our fifth child. Our second home is only 1,350 square feet and is laid out to suit us well. By purchasing the smallest possible house to meet our needs, we still have flexibility to make further changes in our lifestyle without major financial strain.

Principle #2: *Stay Out of Debt*

Ideally, none of us would have any debt at all. Realistically, most of us have at least a mortgage on our home. It is a good investment of your money to prepay on your mortgage whenever possible. Larry Burkett says, "The best recommendation I can give to anyone is this: pay back what you borrow and never borrow frivolously."[5] It is common to hear people talk about investments and the best opportunity for financial gain. I believe that until you have paid off your mortgage, there is no better investment than to prepay on that loan. A biblical principle undergirds this advice: "The rich rule over the poor, and the borrower is servant to the lender" (Proverbs 22:7). No matter how much money you make in other investments, if you have a mortgage outstanding, you are at risk when unemployment comes unexpectedly. Middle management has seen a significantly greater incidence of layoffs in recent years as companies are reorganizing and downscaling. Periods of unemployment are more manageable when you are debt-free.

Other types of debt are to be avoided if you wish to simplify your life. As a mortgage loan processor I processed many loans in the early 1980s that were evidence of lifestyles of debt that I had never seen before. It was common for a couple to have two or three VISA cards with a combined outstanding balance of $10,000 or more. Credit cards are only a good idea for emergencies or possibly convenience when ordering something over the phone. They should be paid in full every month. Even during our most difficult financial times, we did not carry a balance on our VISA. If we had, I believe we would have continued to carry a balance.

This will seem like a radically different way of thinking (and it is) at first, but determine in your family not to borrow for *anything* except the home mortgage. When we came to this conclusion, our decision was tested in a challenging way. We were returning from a trip to an outlet mall when our Volkswagon Vanagon caught fire. It was an older model with a fairly new engine, and it had been giving us problems all summer. My husband does almost all of our car repairs, and after working on it for quite some time he decided to take it to the dealership to fix one more problem that had him baffled. I had found myself stranded in this van with the kids on more than one occasion, and I was ready for a new van.

Before Jim took the van to the dealer, I asked him to go out on a Saturday afternoon to "just look" at used vans to see if what we wanted was available at a used car lot anywhere. It probably seemed silly to him to even do this since we had decided we would save cash to purchase a twelve-passenger van to replace our old VW. After searching the lots we found nothing, until we passed a dealer on the way home and noticed "the perfect van" sitting on the lot. Inspection of the vehicle determined that it would indeed meet our needs beautifully and was also priced well.

We went home heavy of heart since we did not yet have the cash saved up. We took our old van in to get it fixed, and when it was returned to us we decided to just drive it until it died, which it did three days later. Fortunately, we had already found a replacement and promptly went to purchase it. We borrowed against equity in our home to pay for it. This was not our plan, but by refinancing our home a short time later, we were able to get rid of our car debt.

Principle #3: Refinance

I have already shared how refinancing our home helped us in two ways. We were able to separate our tax liability from our mortgage payment. This not only helps to lower monthly mortgage payments but allows you to keep your tax money in an account and earn interest on that money instead of the lender who will be holding it in escrow until the tax bill is due. Lenders also collect a little more than the expected tax bill to cover themselves in case the bill increases more than expected (doesn't that happen often!). Just be sure you budget for the tax bill that is due so you are prepared. I will share more about budgets in a later chapter. We were also able to use the equity in our home to finance an emergency (our van catching fire, making it necessary to purchase another vehicle).

Refinancing saves you money when the prevailing interest rates are at least 2 percent lower than your current loan. Even though we refinanced our first home twice in nine and a half years, we saved in many respects. Rates dropped from about 14 percent when we purchased the home to about 7 percent for a fixed rate when we moved. The cost of refinancing was more than offset by the interest savings we enjoyed. Even though each time you refinance you usually extend the life of the loan (for example, if you have a thirty-year loan and refinance after two years to another thirty-year loan, it is as if you are starting over), we chose to shorten our term on the last refinance. Because rates had come down so low, we were able to go with a twenty-year mortgage. Mike Yorkey advises, "Generally speaking, making one extra loan payment a year will reduce a thirty year mortgage to seventeen years."[6] Many options are available to you, and it pays to be informed. Speak to a knowledgeable loan officer where you do your banking to understand your options should you need to exercise them.

Principle #4: Rethink the Use of Medical Services

When I was a child and I was sick, I was taken to the doctor. We had an older man who was our family practice physician. In those days, if your condition did not warrant any aggressive treatment (such as a penicillin shot), you simply went home and let nature take its course. It is not that way in our day. Because of the type of malpractice suits being won in our nation, doctors are more wary of sending away a patient without some type of treatment. Many doctors will send patients away with antibiotics when their conditions are viral. Antibiotics do not clear up viral infections and in fact have a negative impact on our system (the killing of all bacteria, even the good bacteria, which often leads to a yeast infection while a person is taking antibiotics). Antibiotics should be taken with care and used only when necessary. We are also seeing superstrains of bacteria that are resistant to antibiotics. Research has indicated that overuse of antibiotics has contributed to this problem.

Doctors also prescribe many more tests than when I was a child. While many of them are good, they have come to be accepted as routine in areas where caution should be exercised. Amniocentesis has become very popular in our day regardless of its risks. Should a defect be found in the child through this test, moral questions of pregnancy termination are initiated. This is objectionable on several counts.

We have found it prudent to develop a relationship with a family practice physician who understands and respects our philosophies. He supports natural childbirth and has been a trusted resource. We did not follow routine procedures in the births of our last three children. We avoided practices that made my labors long and difficult with my first two children. We test only when necessary and have been blessed by his refusal to prescribe antibiotics for illness that is obviously viral in nature.

A doctor who knows you may also offer you a reduced cost for his services during times of financial hardship. We try only to visit our doctor for illness that truly requires medical attention. We phone first and describe our symptoms so he can determine if we need to be seen. The viruses in our day are so strong that, based on how sick we feel, it often seems like we should be hospitalized but don't necessarily need to be. Recently I was in bed for four days straight (I don't sit still that long even after giving birth). I knew from talking to friends that my symptoms were much like a virus that was going around. Still, I felt so bad that I visited the doctor. My eye was infected as well, and he gave me some drops since he diagnosed it as bacterial. A few days later it was no better, and I went to an eye specialist who informed me that it was viral and would probably last another week. Even though I felt very ill, my problems were not such that a doctor could help me.

While there is nothing wrong with going to the doctor for our symptoms, it should not be our first inclination to run to the doctor with everything. It is wise to be informed about our bodies and how to care for them. When medical services are necessary, it is our responsibility to know what is being done and why. I will expand on health concerns in the next chapter.

Principle #5: Bring Dad Home More

This will be a lower-income alternative if Dad is not making as much money because he is home. Then again, home businesses are so popular now that it may be possible to increase your income with Dad at home. Whatever your situation, it is good for the family to have Dad around. That sounds trite, but in our culture there are many children who do not even see their father before they go to bed because he is not home from work yet. If this is your arrangement, you may want to consider the benefits of another job for Dad.

There is no substitute for the relationship that children have with their father. (If due to death or divorce there is no father in your home, take heart—"The Lord watches over the alien and sustains the fatherless and the widow," Psalm 146:9.) The years of childhood are brief, and if Dad waits until the teenage years to spend time with the children, his influence will face fierce competition. A Christian father's role with his children is given in

Deuteronomy 6:6-7: "These commandments that I give you today are to be upon your hearts. Impress them on your children. Talk about them when you sit at home and when you walk along the road, when you lie down and when you get up." This will be very difficult to do if Dad is working sixty hours a week.

Principle #6: Less Stuff—More Relationship

I hardly feel qualified to discuss getting rid of clutter. I still have not conquered in this area. I do know that our family is rethinking many of our possessions. At my friend Lori's advice, we are looking at the quality of an item's use rather than the quantity of items to use.[7] Our desire is to spend less money and spend more emotion, time, and energy on being with our family. I cannot do this if I am always having to clean up piles of things or to find a place to store something new.

Scripture is full of advice in this area, and we would do well to heed the warnings. "Then he said to them, 'Watch out! Be on your guard against all kinds of greed; a man's life does not consist in the abundance of his possessions" (Luke 12:15). "Turn my eyes away from worthless things; renew my life according to your word" (Psalm 119:37). In a later chapter I will elaborate on how to go about deciding what to get rid of and what to keep.

Principle #7: Cut Back on the Budget

When there is more income available to a family, the typical response is to increase spending by that amount. Often a family will buy a larger home because they can now afford one, even if they do not really need it. I suggest planning to *not* increase your spending. As we are blessed with more children, we are not planning on raising the food budget. While there may come a time when we must make a change, our goal is to find more economical ways to feed the family. It is too tempting to just spend more if more money is available.

We have purposed for a number of years now to reduce our expenses rather than look for ways to increase our income. Our wood-burning stove is but one example. It has been a slow process, but it is working. My husband's salary is low for the area that we live in and for the size of our family; yet we are living quite comfortably. There are many more areas in which we can cut our spending, and we are working on them one at a time.

Principle #8: *Cook from Scratch*

This principle not only saves on the cost of food but also on medical expenses. Since we have been eating more healthily, we have not had to deal with illness nearly so often. Prepackaged food is less nutritious, more expensive, and often has chemical additives that make it a poor choice. There are ways to streamline cooking from scratch that make it almost as easy as cooking from a box. I will elaborate on this in the chapter on food.

Principle #9: *Save on Utilities*

This has been a difficult area for me to change. We recently had one of the hottest Midwestern summers in quite a few years, and we only ran our air conditioning for a handful of days. We just had to slow down our pace (and that is not a bad idea!) and realize our limitations in the heat. I would rather be productive and "get something done" each day, but that is not always possible. I am now going to plan for every summer to be hot and expect to accomplish less during that time. When the savings realized from not running the air conditioning amount to hundreds of dollars, I can't afford to have any other plan.

Heating our home has been a steadily decreasing cost as well.

Just last winter I invested in a down comforter and some flannel sheets that are really very warm at night. With the approaching winter we are anxious to see how much we save with our wood-burning stove. All our wood was free and actually was delivered to our backyard by a tree trimmer. My husband cut and split the wood over the summer, resulting in approximately eight cords of wood stacked and ready to go. Based on the prices of seasoned wood in our area, we have determined the value of this wood to be $1,800. I find that exciting!

We also conserve water by not bathing every day. Summer months often necessitate a daily bath, but a small pool in the backyard can accomplish the same thing. I also minimize the laundry I do in hot water. This way you are not paying to heat the water. I have found that even soiled blue jeans come clean in cold water. It is also a good idea to turn down the temperature on your hot water heater. This is safer for children and helps trim the budget. I recommend shutting off the hot water in some locations of your home. But make sure you and your husband are in agreement over this. Jim is very frugal, and one day I found there was no hot water in the sink in the children's bathroom. He reasoned that the children would turn on the hot water and let it run too long. He did not realize that this was where I washed my hands after changing cloth diapers. Determining what will work for your own family is a trial and error process that takes understanding from both parties. There is no right or wrong way to live simply. You need to find out what works for you.

We have also purchased some oil lamps. The Fahey homestead did not have electricity, and we enjoyed their oil lamps. Oil lamps have a way of attracting the entire family to the room where they are located. For a couple of years now we have used an oil lamp at our dinner table in the wintertime. At first I was frustrated with it (notice that it is always me that seems to have a hard time adjusting). I like to see my food! After a while we put two lamps on the table, and now I like it very much. We try to go to bed early, so the lamps are on a short time each day. We do use our lights as well, but our children are taught to turn them off when they are not needed. We also discourage the children from turning lights on during the day when the sun is out. It helps to have a home with many windows.

Principle #10: Go to Garage Sales

I know that not all parts of the country have such wonderful garage sales as we do here in the western suburbs of Chicago. For those of you who do have this opportunity, I highly recommend that you take advantage of them. I have a long list of unbelievable buys I have found at garage sales. Finding children's clothing with the tags still on is now commonplace. Each winter I begin a list of the items I will need to look for the next summer. By the end of the season I usually have crossed everything off my list. Beware of "bargains" that will only become clutter in your home. I know I am guilty of some of these. For the discerning economizer, there are great benefits to garage and yard sales.

Principle #11: Bake Your Own Bread

As I shared at the beginning, my first attempts at bread making were not all that great. What kept me going was how good homemade bread tasted. I did not even know about the nutritional benefits or how economical it would be. With a good recipe and the right equipment (a Kitchen Aid Mixer or larger mixers such as the Bosch Universal or Magic Mill DLX), it is not difficult to make bread. I would not recommend bread machines because they only make one loaf at a time and have average results. If you own one, by all means use it and benefit from homemade bread. If not, I will be covering equipment in a later chapter.

Principle #12: *Make Capital Investments*

In business it is not unusual to hear that you have to "spend money to make money." In our home we have found that we have to "spend money to *save* money." Before we moved out of our first home, we made a list of all the capital investments we wanted to make. Our investments were not in stocks and bonds or mutual funds but in equipment that would help us provide for our own needs. Some of the items on our list included a serger sewing machine, a grain mill, a Magic Mill DLX mixer, a computer, and a pop-up camper (how else does a large family afford to travel?). The purpose behind the list was to identify what was most important and then to acquire these things as funds became available. We were making one-time purchases of tools that would help us accomplish our tasks.

In an unbelievably short time we found that all of the items on our list had been provided in one way or another. This was a great blessing to us since we do not believe that our nation will be financially prosperous indefinitely. The experts have been talking about hard financial times ahead, and we want to get the tools we need now. For more on this very real possibility, you might want to read *The Coming Economic Earthquake* by Larry Burkett.

Principle #13: *Prepare for Hard Times*

The money crunch is inevitable. The best way to prepare is to minimize debt, improve health via lifestyle changes, and acquire the tools you will need to provide for more of your own needs. Let your needs be known since some of what you are looking for, people are currently throwing out. We can and freeze produce and have received dozens of jars and other canning supplies from people who no longer are interested in canning. After having 32,000 pounds of logs delivered to our backyard, the very next day I found a good chain saw at a garage sale. Know what you need, and go after it while you can.

Principle #14: *Budget Your Time*

Most of us know the value of budgets for our money (we will discuss this further later). But how many of us budget our time? Do you know anyone who believes they have enough time? I don't. We are a very busy culture, just bustling with activity day and night. It is essential that we make good decisions about how we spend our time. We need to have criteria set up for our family to help us evaluate each request for our time. Does it further the Lord's work? Does it enhance my family life? Does this activity prepare my child for life? Does this commitment take me away from the family too much? The list is endless. It is no longer possible to merely pick out *good* activities and commitments. They must be the *best*. We don't have time for all that is offered to us.

A favorite Scripture passage keeps me on track in this area: "And this is my prayer: that your love may abound more and more in knowledge and depth of insight, so that you may be able to discern what is best and may be pure and blameless until the day of Christ" (Philippians 1:9-10). Unless we discern what is best, we will be on overload. Our children need to learn this early on since the world they live in demands many more choices than we had when we were growing up. Alvin Toffler alerted us to the concept of overchoice back in 1970 in his book *Future Shock*: "If we also assume that the shift toward superindustrialism will multiply the kinds and complexities of decisions facing the individual, it becomes apparent that education must address the issue of overchoice directly."[8] I remember reading that book in high school and thinking that even then there were too many choices. That is certainly the case today.

It is helpful to post your family schedule so everyone in the family can visualize the time commitments for the week. We have a dry-erase calendar on our refrigerator. At each meal we can all see what is on it. I color-code activities by who is doing them. It is thus easy to see if someone has overbooked for the week. Even with this system it is a struggle to manage our time well because of the many options open to us. Each week I put up "STAY HOME" in my color for two or three days. If I am to be a homemaker, then I need to be home. Errands can be run on certain days. On my "STAY HOME" days, if something comes up I can say no.

Principle #15: Do It Yourself

Don't pay others to do what you can do for yourself. There are certain situations where it will be better to pay someone, but it is not necessary if you have the ability to do it. Lack of time to do something is often a function of putting in too many hours at the office. You end up needing a higher income to pay for the services of other people that you could be providing for yourself. You also rob your children of the opportunity to learn these skills. Just yesterday I saw an ad for a "Multi-purpose Household Management Company." The list of services they provide is a description of the work I do as a homemaker. There was a coupon attached for ten dollars off any service. I would imagine these services are rather costly.

Principle #16: Remember That Your Family Is Unique

Every family is special. I cannot even begin to presume which of my suggestions will help you. That is a decision your family will have to make. I do know that our own journey toward a simpler lifestyle has been both faith-building and exciting.

I have had to change my expectations and have been greatly blessed in the process. Learn to trust the Lord for His provision. You *can* live more simply. You *can* do it yourself. You *can* downscale. Make a wish list of objectives, then focus, save, and plan for them. Change one area of your life at a time if possible. Be encouraged by the possibilities that lay ahead for your family.

2

Healthy Living

HEALTH IS FOUNDATIONAL TO IMPLEMENTING SIMPLE LIVING philosophies. If we are ailing and have multiple afflictions, it will be difficult to work hard with our bodies. Recently I had the unusual circumstance of finding myself bedridden with a debilitating virus. I was fortunate to have my husband home for a few days to run the household. I found it frustrating to lie in bed and think about how to organize the first chapter of this book. I was too sick to sit at the computer to put my thoughts in writing. If I was frequently ill, it would not be possible to make many of the lifestyle changes we are making.

We live in an age when it is difficult to even define what constitutes healthy living. Some would say that an absence of sickness or chronic illness is health. Others would feel healthy if they could reach their "ideal" weight. Many feel that if they can get on their treadmill and do their thirty-minute walk faithfully three times a week, they are in good health. A popular approach to health is to eat a low-fat diet. While all of these definitions have merit, they are too simplistic in nature. Healthy living embodies a lifestyle that facilitates not only physical health, but emotional and spiritual as well.

Spiritual Health

Spiritual health greatly impacts physical and emotional health. Unfortunately, most of us start improving our physical health first and often fail to address our spiritual health. I define spiritual health as a genuine, consistent commitment to a relationship with the Lord Jesus Christ. Through daily devotional times, fellowship with other Christians, church attendance, and meditation on God's Word, I have found that my life has been greatly changed. None of these things in and of themselves guarantees me spiritual health. It is only my commitment to follow Christ (through His teachings in the Bible) that enables me to find peace. In his sermon to the Gentiles in the house of Cornelius, Peter explained this to the people: "I now realize how true it is that God does not show favoritism but accepts men from every nation who fear him and do what is right. This is the message God sent to the people of Israel, telling the good news of peace through Jesus Christ, who is Lord of all" (Acts 10:34-36).

Devotional times have never been easy for me to establish as a routine. I have many children with various needs and have not been able to find a regular time each day to be alone with God. I have finally stopped feeling guilty about this and realize that due to my circumstances I need to approach devotions differently. I encourage you to examine your own life and structure this special time with the Lord to meet your own situation. I believe it is not so important to do your devotions at a specific time as long as you do them regularly. My devotional times have included Bible reading, a specific Bible study I'm working on, prayer during my half-hour brisk walk, and devotional books such as *Heart Throbs of Motherhood*.[1] This devotional book was compiled by a mother of eight children and is a constant source of inspiration to me. There are many such books available. By no means have I reached my goal of doing this every day. But I do see a pattern developing of spending more and more time with the Lord. I see many benefits from this pattern.

Biblical remedies to the trials we face daily are much easier to put into practice when we know what they are. I need to read the Bible to know how I should respond appropriately. I am a calmer person when I have read a Bible-based poem or a story in a devotional book that encourages me in areas of difficulty. Prayer eases the crises of the moment as I cast my cares on the Lord instead of trying to deal with them in my own power.

Taking the time to do a Bible study on my own helps me gain the knowledge and insight I need to do my job. My favorite study is entitled *Homemaking—A Bible Study for Women at Home* by Baukje Doornenbal and Tjitske Lemstra.[2] I began this study just two years after becoming a Christian but did not finish it until three and a half years later. It became a springboard for other areas of study. I did not leave the workforce until my oldest child was born and have been getting my homemaker training "on the job" ever since. This study helped me focus on specific areas that I needed to develop.

Fellowship with other Christians has been a vital source of information and encouragement. Much of what I share in this book is not just what I think but is rather an expression of the experiences, thoughts, and feelings of the many godly women I have had the privilege to know. Often in the midst of a difficulty it is hard for us to stay focused and keep our perspective. I value the opportunity to bounce what I am thinking off others who can offer suggestions from a detached position. The benefits of fellowship are many and can boost your spiritual health greatly.

Attending a particular church and becoming involved in it is an easy way to have fellowship with other Christians. There is a biblical mandate for us to do so: "Let us not give up meeting together, as some are in the habit of doing, but let us encourage one another—and all the more as you see the Day approaching" (Hebrews 10:25). In a culture that tramples on Christian values, it is a breath of fresh air to worship with others who call on Christ as their Lord.

Meditating on God's Word has also brought blessing to me. I used to think that just memorizing a verse would be sufficient and that in a time of need it would just come to mind. While this does happen, I believe that thinking about the verse over and over does more to help us remember and understand the verse. Sometimes there will be a word in the verse that you do not understand and need to look up. There have been times that I did not even notice a word such as this until I had been thinking about the verse for a while.

Please be assured that as I make these suggestions to you, I am making them to myself as well. We all get busy and forget how important these areas are to our spiritual health. I challenge you to look at your schedule and find just a few minutes a day to apply one or two of these suggestions. It may seem trivial, but I believe that unless we attend to our spiritual health first, efforts we make to eat better, exercise more, or whatever else we might do will be less productive.

Emotional Health

Have you ever noticed that the state of your emotions has a lot to do with your ability to do something positive for your physical health? Emotional distress not only creates physical stress for the body, it prevents us from taking care of ourselves. When I am upset, I don't usually feel inclined to exercise (although this would benefit me at that moment), make healthy meals, rest, or do anything else that would help me physically. Instead I am caught up in the feelings of the moment that can wear me down quickly if I do not know how to deal with them appropriately.

The Random House College Dictionary defines *emotion* as "an affective state of consciousness in which joy, sorrow, fear, hate, or the like, is experienced."[3] The same dictionary lists as a definition for *health*, "vigor, vitality."[4] I know that when I am feeling angry, vigor and vitality are not descriptive of my physical condition. Anger has been my "thorn in the flesh" that reminds me of how inadequate I am without the Lord's help. When I allow something or someone to make me angry, I usually feel drained physically. If the situation is not remedied quickly, I may lose my appetite, lose sleep, get a headache, or face other problems. The book of Proverbs has much to say about anger. For example, "A fool gives full vent to his anger, but a wise man keeps himself under control" (29:11). I confess that there are many occasions where I have played the role of a fool. Another passage that encourages me is Ephesians 4:26-27, "'In your anger do not sin': Do not let the sun go down while you are still angry, and do not give the devil a foothold."

As I have purposed to apply these verses in my life, I have found that whatever has made me angry does not have control over me like it did when I used to let things brew in my mind for days. Another passage I am appreciating more and more is found in James: "My dear brothers, take note of this: Everyone should be quick to listen, slow to speak and slow to become angry, for man's anger does not bring about the righteous life that God desires" (1:19-20).

Anger is but one emotion that can take away our emotional health. Other attitudes that also rob us include selfishness, pride, arrogance, greed, envy, a critical spirit, hatred, and jealousy, to name a few. Each one of us has at least one area in our lives that wears us down emotionally. It may be that you are consumed with fear about the future, which manifests itself in constant worrying about everything. Paul writes in his letter to the Philippians, "Do not be anxious about anything, but in everything, by prayer and petition, with thanksgiving, present your requests to God" (Philippians 4:6).

Whatever your weak area may be, the Scriptures have a solution for you. In applying what I said previously about the importance of reading the Bible, you are actually providing a means of nurturing your emotional health. Counseling, therapy, and the like are popular today. While they do have their place, I believe that many of the answers we seek to our relationship problems are found right in the Scriptures.

Emotions are sometimes powerful indicators of what we hide in our hearts. I want my life to manifest the fruit of the Spirit—"love, joy, peace, patience, kindness, goodness, faithfulness, gentleness and self-control" (Galatians 5:22). In order to achieve this goal, I am committed to making devotions, fellowship with other Christians, church attendance, and meditating on God's Word priorities in my life. We are all busy, but surely there is a space on our calendar to mark off personal time that will be an opportunity to build our emotional health.

Physical Health

Self-help books that claim to teach us how to be healthy are everywhere. Magazines, newspapers, and radio and TV talk shows regularly address our desire to learn more about how to keep our bodies healthy. With so much information at our disposal, why are we so ill? Why are there so many degenerative illnesses?

The difficulty many of us have with the information available on our physical health is that it is presented in ways that make it hard for us to integrate the information into the big picture. We hear much about the need to keep the fat in our diet regulated or to limit our salt intake. These statements are true but incomplete by themselves. We also need to consider that replacing fats and salt with artificial ingredients is merely trading one problem for another. We cannot possibly remember all of the do's and don'ts of good health if they are not explained in a way we can implement. I know I should exercise, but just how am I to do that with my busy schedule? The problem becomes further complicated by the fact that the "experts" regularly disagree about what we should do with our bodies. I have on more than one occasion read conflicting information from two people whom I respect.

I would like to encourage you to overcome some of these problems by developing a new mind-set about your physical health. We must start with acknowledging the source of our physical bodies. "For you created my inmost being; you knit me together in my mother's womb. I praise you because I am fearfully and wonderfully made; your works are wonderful, I know that full well. My frame was not hidden from you when I was made in the secret place. When I was woven together in the depths of the earth, your eyes saw my unformed body. All the days ordained for me were written in your book before one of them came to be" (Psalm 139:13-16). It is humbling to realize that God in His infinite wisdom made us just the way He wanted us, so we could accomplish the purpose He ordained for us here on earth.

I admit that I do not always appreciate the way God made me. I don't mind being short, but I really think it would be nice to be a little slimmer. (OK, sometimes I wish I were a lot slimmer!) Just last night my husband and I were going through our clothing together in the hope that maybe we could encourage each other to get rid of some of it (getting rid of clutter is a constant process). I had given Jim a pair of jeans I had worn in college. He was now getting rid of them. Just for fun I decided to try them on. Big mistake! Even though I weigh only ten pounds more than I did then, it was amazing to see just how small those jeans were. I also had to give away most of my belts. I could easily have had a pity party and planned on starving myself for a few days, but neither of these responses would have been appropriate.

What came to mind as I was taking off the jeans was that at that time I had given birth to five children in eight years. Naturally my waistline can prove it! God has blessed me with the ability to bear children. My body serves very well in that capacity. Just because I don't have the same physical dimensions I did fifteen years ago doesn't mean I need to actively pursue getting them back. Once we accept the way God has designed our own particular physical body, we can nourish and take care of it properly. It helps to remember that our body is God's temple: "Don't you know that you yourselves are God's temple and that God's Spirit lives in you? If anyone destroys God's temple, God will destroy him; for God's temple is sacred, and you are that temple" (1 Corinthians 3:16-17).

I do have a commitment to exercise. Even though I do not anticipate ever seeing my college figure again, I can still make efforts to keep my weight at a satisfactory level. There are many benefits of regular exercise. Because our bodies have been designed for physical exercise, the heart, lungs, circulatory system, and the other systems in our bodies function better with exercise. Earlier in history when push-button, labor-saving devices were not available, people did physical work while fulfilling their day-to-day responsibilities. Today the Amish still benefit from using hand tools, plowing with horses, hanging clothes on the line, and gardening. The summer before this writing, Jim enjoyed swinging the axe to cut and split his firewood. I have enjoyed the fresh air when hanging clothes on the line on a sunny day. In our family we take the opportunity to do manual labor whenever possible. While I do use and enjoy many modern conveniences, I realize that in order to get enough exercise, I must create the opportunities to do so.

Aerobic exercise is a good choice for physical health. It increases your intake of oxygen, which will benefit your heart and lungs. It is generally accepted that to do twenty minutes to half an hour of aerobic exercise three times a week will be enough to strengthen our cardiovascular system. Many health-care professionals suggest every day if possible. When we had two children, I found it reasonable to get to a health club on a fairly regular basis. Now I get my exercise by walking alone for half an hour per day. (This is the plan anyway.) I would love to do this every day, but in reality I usually take my brisk walk two to three times per week (just before lunch on the days my husband is off-duty from the firehouse). After a busy morning of home school-ing, the walk helps clear my head and prepare me for the afternoon. I take this time to pray, which elevates my spiritual health. If I am experiencing stress, my emotional health benefits from the walk too.

Exercise stimulates the release of endorphins (hormones that are located in the pituitary gland) that have a calming effect on my body. Those who work full-time could benefit from taking part of their lunch hour to take a brisk walk. Other forms of aer-obic activity such as swimming, bicycling, cross-country skiing, hiking, and jumping rope are good choices. (But use caution if you like to run since running can be hard on the muscles and joints.)

The commitment to regular exercise is important to our phys-ical health. We also need to take time to rest regularly. When I worked in an office, we had two coffee breaks each day and usu-ally went out somewhere for lunch. These were built-in times of rest during my workday. I had the opportunity to stop my work for a time and think about something else. In my work as a homemaker, I do not experience rest during my day unless I schedule it in.

I wonder if the following scenario describes your life as it does mine. You get up before the desired wake-up time in the morning (one of the children woke up early) and hastily dress yourself so you can help the other children who are waking. At some point you begin "the schedule" for your family. Whether taking your children to day care or school or starting your day of home school on time, the pace of the morning rush hour usually leaves you out of breath. The details of the morning pass by so quickly that lunch is already just a few minutes away. You have not been doing less than two things at a time all morning.

Somewhere during the afternoon there needs to be a time for rest. I confess that I have not implemented this advice yet. I am writing this book during the afternoon hours. The thought of losing just fifteen minutes of time bothers me. But why is that? Must we always be on the move? Do we have to maximize every waking minute? I often believe this to be true. But if we look beyond the demands of the moment, we can see that we are actually more productive if we stop to take a rest. Harvey and Marilyn Diamond are speaking directly to me in their book *Living Health* when they discuss rest: "What is rest? It is a period of inactivity during which the body can restore expended energy. When we've depleted our energies faster than they can be restored, a period of inactivity enables the body to catch up."[5] I need this period of inactivity every day, and yet rarely do I take it. I am convicted as I write this to make rest a priority in my day. The Diamonds offer suggestions as to how we can rejuvenate ourselves through rest:

There are four kinds of rest that can be used to replenish and refresh oneself.

1. Physical rest may be obtained by discontinuing physical activity—sitting or lying down and relaxing.

2. Sensory rest is secured by quiet and by refraining from using the eyes, which curtails a great drain of energy.

3. Emotional rest is achieved by withdrawing from involvement in the ups and downs caused by personal interaction.

4. Mental rest is obtained by detaching the mind from any and all intellectual demands or activity.[6]

All of us know the results of not taking time out to rest. We are crabby, the children become crabby, we all crab at Daddy when he comes through the door. Peak fatigue time in a mother's day is often around 4 P.M. If the preceding hour could be a more restful time for you and your children, it might be that the difficult times experienced during dinner preparation could be minimized. Children need a few minutes to rest as much as we do. Taking fifteen minutes or so to sit down and be together may be just the calming influence everyone needs. On days when the children want to talk, just let them talk to you. Even though your mind is still working, wouldn't it be a blessing to lie on the floor or couch for fifteen minutes? Some of you must be wondering how a person can be so busy he or she can't even rest for fifteen minutes. It doesn't take a large family to keep a mom busy. I believe too many of us are racing from one activity to the next without giving ourselves or our children a rest.

Even if we do a fairly good job of regular exercise and rest, there is another component of physical health that requires close examination. What are we doing for our family regarding feeding them a proper diet? Trying to establish a proper diet for my family has probably taken more time than anything else I will cover in this book. It has required many hours of research to educate myself in this area, and I feel as though I have only scratched the surface. Much information exists on diet, but so much of it is specialized and leaves the reader to figure out how it all fits together. One excellent comprehensive book is *Healthy Habits— 20 Simple Ways to Improve Your Health* by David and Anne Frahm. Anne was dying of breast cancer at the age of thirty-six. Doctors had exhausted all of the possible treatments and determined her case to be terminal. In their quest to save Anne's life, the Frahms discovered incredible results from a nutritional approach to building up Anne's immune system. Tests later revealed that the cancer was gone.

Our family's approach to health is to build up the immune system. While we are not battling terminal illness, we are committed to chronic wellness. We strongly believe that the improved health we have enjoyed in recent years is directly related to the dietary and lifestyle changes that we are making as a family. As I sift through new thoughts on diet and lifestyle, I focus on moderation. The "experts" regularly disagree, and I don't see much benefit in adhering to the opinions of those who are on the far right or far left side of an issue. At times we have decided to eliminate items from our diet completely, but that does not mean you must do the same. I will share why we have made the choices we've made, and you can decide if your family can benefit from our experience. The process of dietary change is a slow and steady one. We are not fanatics, but simply a family desiring to be healthy. The following topics are in no way exhaustive, and should questions be raised in your mind, I would encourage you to do further research. This is the process by which we ourselves are learning.

It will be helpful to understand the 1992 USDA Food Guide Pyramid before we examine specific dietary changes. The USDA first issued a food guide in 1916, called *Food for Young Children*. In 1946 the public schools and public health workers were teaching the Basic Seven Food Groups. These included:

1. Leafy green and yellow vegetables.
2. Citrus fruit, tomatoes, raw cabbage.
3. Potatoes and other vegetables and fruits.
4. Milk, cheese, and ice cream.
5. Meat, poultry, fish, eggs, dried peas, and beans.
6. Bread, flour, cereals, whole-grain or enriched.
7. Butter or fortified margarine.

It is interesting to note that while it was common practice to plan meals around these guidelines, changes in attitudes about illness began to shift how these guidelines were implemented. "The prevailing wisdom in the fifties, and for several decades thereafter: drugs are used to treat illnesses; food is necessary to sustain life and to promote growth and reproduction. Following the example of the USDA guidelines, textbook publishers did not offer suggestions regarding foods which caused disease or foods which cured disease. The Basic Seven food choices were presented as seven different, but equally important categories."[7] By the time I entered school in the mid-sixties, there were the Basic Four Food Groups. These included:

1. The Milk Group
2. The Meat Group
3. The Fruit and Vegetable Group
4. The Bread and Cereal Group

1992 USDA FOOD GUIDE PYRAMID
A GUIDE TO DAILY FOOD CHOICES

FATS, OILS,
& SWEETS
Use Sparingly

MILK, YOGURT,
& CHEESE GROUP
2-3 Servings

MEAT, POULTRY, FISH,
DRY BEANS, EGGS & NUTS GROUP
2-4 Servings

FRUIT GROUP
2-4 Servings

VEGETABLE GROUP
3-5 Servings

BREAD, CEREAL, RICE & PASTA GROUP
6-11 Servings

Based on what I was taught, I understood that to eat foods from each of these four groups daily would provide my body with all I would need.

Finally, in 1992 the USDA came up with a food guide pyramid that is substantially different in its organization. All food groups do not have the same emphasis but are presented in the form of a pyramid.

Notice that the meat group includes poultry, fish, dry beans, eggs, and nuts. Yogurt and cheese are included in the milk group. Fruits and vegetables as well as grains are emphasized in this pyramid.[8] For further detailed information on this pyramid, I suggest the *Eating Better Program Guide* by Teresa Ann Dorian, Ph.D., available through Nutriflex, 800-888-8587. The dietary changes we have made as a family line up better with this new guideline than they do with the way most of us were taught to eat.

Just how does a family decide what to change in their diet anyway? I suggest to you that it will depend on your own individual family. If, for instance, you frequent fast-food establishments, it may be prudent to just commit to limiting these visits, an expensive, poor nutritional choice for feeding the family. In the next chapter I will share ways to be prepared for meals when you are out so fast food is not necessary. Even though the fast-food chains are promoting low-fat and other seemingly healthy selections, don't be fooled. Fast food is not a good source of nutrition. If your family eats red meat every day, this is an easy area to consider modifying. If sodas, chips, and other junk foods are regular family snacks, this is another area that lends itself to change.

While these examples are fairly obvious, other changes you might not yet know about can also be made to improve your health. As I share some of our dietary changes with you, bear in mind that these were gradual changes. We do not eat a pristine diet, nor do we faithfully adhere to what we know is healthy eating 100 percent of the time. It is our desire to modify our diet as we become aware of areas that should be reassessed. Sometimes

I have become aware of a problem but did not understand it completely; so we did not make a change until I read further information.

Be encouraged that you can make a difference in your family's health by modifying your diet. I know that even though we are a large family, we seldom see our doctor. He is a friend and tells us when we do visit that he misses our family. Can you imagine being so healthy that your doctor misses seeing you?

One very important decision we have made is to drink pure water. At first we filled empty jugs at the store with purified water. This became cumbersome until we contracted with a service to bring it to our home. Once we moved, we installed a reverse-osmosis system under the kitchen sink.

Suburban Chicago waited many years for a pipeline to be built so Lake Michigan water could be piped out to us. Our water bills rose to cover the cost of the pipeline. Although most of us were able to disconnect our water softeners because of the Lake Michigan water, that was a mixed blessing. At first we thought it tasted just fine. We visited a water treatment plant about twenty minutes from our home that explained how the lake water was treated to make it "safe to drink." We took all of this in without much questioning. Time passed, and I noticed that when I took a shower, the bathroom smelled like a swimming pool. If the chlorine smell was so strong, what did that mean when we drank the water? I did some investigating and discovered they had increased the amount of chlorine to treat the water after a water problem in Milwaukee had made many people ill.

Based on the chlorine issue alone, we decided to go to bottled water. This created an expense for us that we had not incurred before, but we did not want to consume all of that chlorine. As I researched safe drinking water for this chapter, I learned that there is even more to be concerned about with our drinking water. In our area chlorine is the biggest issue, so we thought. I now know that solder that is half lead and half tin has been used widely in plumbing in our area. The lead leaches into the drinking water. Because hot water dissolves more lead from pipes than cold water does, it is a good idea to use only cold water for cooking and drinking. Run the faucet briefly before taking any water so that if any lead has accumulated, you won't be using it. I also wonder about the spread of microbes in the water since "new evidence suggests conventional treatment procedures are not working. Some microbes are resistant to the chemical, and others are tiny enough to slither through filters."[9] If parasites in drinking water are resistant to chlorine, they can make us sick. "Researchers in Montreal recently found that one third of gastrointestinal illnesses were caused by drinking water and are preventable."[10]

In addition to chlorine, lead, and microbes, there are concerns about nitrates and radon. These concerns generally pertain to private wells and, in the case of radon, "community water systems serving fewer than 500 people."[11] Problems with nitrates usually come from contamination of groundwater. "Chemical fertilizers and manure from animal feed lots are particularly rich sources of nitrogen compounds, which are converted to nitrate in the soil. The nitrate readily migrates into ground water."[12] Although harmful effects of radon gas are commonly known, there are effects from radon in household water. Waterborne radon occurs when showering, washing dishes, or doing laundry. If the air tests high in radon at your home, be sure to test the water as well as if you use groundwater (private wells).

The most prevalent problem with chlorine, lead, and radon are their carcinogenic properties. Nitrates pose problems for infants. I recommend that you read "Fit To Drink?," *Consumer Reports*, January 1990 and "Is Your Water Safe?," *U.S. News and World Report*, July 29, 1991 for further specific information. Many water purification systems exist on the market today and might warrant some consideration for your family. Those having private wells should be sure to have them tested regularly. Wells in agricultural areas are particularly at risk.

In addition to the health risks associated with pesticides leaking into the groundwater, there are risks of contamination on the food we eat. Fresh fruits and vegetables should always be washed and peeled. Many fruits and vegetables that you buy at the store have been waxed. This protective coating often has fungicides mixed in with it, or the wax is covering fungicides on the produce. Fungicides are used to keep the produce from spoiling while it is being shipped and stored; some are suspected carcinogens. In general, we eliminate most of the hazards by washing and peeling our food. A good book that devotes an entire chapter to pesticides is *Everyday Cancer Risks and How to Avoid Them* by Mary Kerney Levenstein. Although it is most desirable to use organic foods, we find they are just too cost-prohibitive to use 100 percent of the time. I primarily buy organic produce and grain (that which is not grown using synthetic fertilizers and pesticides). Fruits and vegetables that we grow ourselves are done organically. A great magazine to help in this endeavor is *Organic Gardening*.

We also avoid additives and preservatives in our food. I suffer from headaches that we have traced in part to additives such as sodium nitrate and sodium nitrite in deli meats, hot dogs, and other foods. Research is continually revealing adverse effects from food additives and preservatives, and we have chosen to avoid them. If you read food labels, you will realize that most prepackaged food contains additives and/or preservatives. To work with this problem, we have decided to cook from scratch in our home. I will be sharing in the next chapter that this is not as difficult as it may sound.

Another major dietary adjustment was to make our own bread from freshly milled grain. Initially I made bread, two loaves at a time, in a Kitchen Aid mixer. I just bought whole wheat flour at the store and felt that we were eating very good bread. Before

The Busy Mom's Guide to Simple Living

50

long I learned from many sources that the wheat flour I purchased at the store had little nutritive value. Most of the nutritive value of the wheat berry is removed in the commercial milling process. The wheat germ is removed, even in "whole wheat" flour because the wheat germ oil becomes rancid so quickly and the flour would have virtually no shelf life. "Ninety percent of the nutritional value of the wheat berry is contained in the wheat germ."[13]

Eventually we were able to purchase a grain mill so we could mill our own fresh flour at home. We also went ahead and bought a larger mixer so I could knead five or six loaves of bread at a time in the mixer. I will be discussing these machines in a later chapter. When people ask me what I believe has made the most difference in improving our health, I must conclude that pure water and home-baked whole grain bread made with freshly milled flour are the top two. We made both of these changes at about the same time and experienced a significant increase in wellness at our house.

A couple of years ago we decided to stop buying pork and beef. My husband's family has a history of heart disease. Since the leading cause of death for a firefighter is a heart attack, we decided to take some preventative measures primarily for my husband's sake. Beef and pork are high in saturated fats as well as containing cholesterol. The saturated fat stimulates the liver to produce more cholesterol, which clogs the arteries. Saturated fats are the type of fat you want to minimize in your diet. I have also learned that medical research has shown that high protein diets (true of regular meat eaters) contribute to calcium loss in our body. I will explain this further when I discuss milk. We choose to eat these turkey and chicken in moderation because they are lower in saturated fat.

At first it was not easy to give up the meat we had been eating all our lives. Our family enjoyed ham and pork chops and ate a fair amount of burgers too! Because we were able to trace some of my headaches to the nitrates and nitrites that are found in pork, we were motivated to give it up. Beef was more difficult because my husband did not really like the taste of ground turkey. With time he grew to like it better, and I found a spice mixture that perks up its flavor. In the back of *The 15 Minute Meal Planner* by Emilie Barnes and Sue Gregg, there is a recipe collection that includes "Ground Turkey Seasoning Mix." This recipe makes enough to season forty-eight pounds of ground turkey.

1. Blend together thoroughly and store in tightly covered labeled container in kitchen cupboard:

   2 Tablespoons nutmeg
   2 Tablespoons thyme leaves
   2 Tablespoons garlic powder
   2 Tablespoons sage

2. Use 1/2 teaspoon seasoning mix per pound.

*Label the container: "Use 1/2 teaspoon per 1 lb., 2 tablespoons catsup, and 1 tablespoon soy sauce."[14]

These same authors have an alternative to using straight butter. They blend one stick of lightly salted butter (very soft) with half a cup of canola oil. This should be refrigerated in a covered container. This stays spreadable directly from the refrigerator.[15] We have preferred to continue using butter in our family after discovering that margarine is no better than butter for your health. Margarine contains trans-fatty acids that are created when heat is used in the processing of the margarine. "Trans-fatty acids are formed when food manufacturers convert liquid vegetable oils into shortening or margarine which are solid or semi-solid at room temperature. Although these products are typically made from soybean, cottonseed, canola, and corn oils, they act like saturated fats."[16] We prefer to use "the real thing" in moderation.

After many years of confusion about all the different types of oils on the market, we have decided to use canola and extra virgin olive oil in our home. The same holds true for oil as it does for meat regarding which type of fat to eliminate. Saturated fats are the type of fat you want to keep to a minimum in your diet. I used safflower oil for some time before understanding why canola is better. Safflower oil is the lowest in saturated fats of the polyunsaturated fats. Of the oils that are polyunsaturated, safflower was the best. The problem with polyunsaturated fats is that they are sensitive to light, heat, and oxygen. Canola and extra virgin olive oil are monounsaturated fats and are not as affected by light, heat, and oxygen. This quality makes monounsaturated oils a better choice. Monounsaturated fats also lower "bad" cholesterol (LDL), without lowering the "good" cholesterol (HDL).

It is a good idea to buy your oil in containers that are not transparent in order to minimize the negative effects of light on the oil. Although this may seem confusing, let's simplify the decision-making process at the store. Minimize your saturated fats (butter, palm kernel oils, coconut oils), buy monounsaturated fats (canola oil, extra virgin olive oil), and minimize your use of polyunsaturated fats (safflower oil, corn oil, sunflower seed oil). I have successfully eliminated oil from my whole wheat bread and substitute unsweetened applesauce for half or more of the oil in quick breads. With a little creativity you can do much to reduce your intake of saturated fats found in oils.

We have made some changes that were easy. Getting rid of the saltshaker was one of them. We figured that salt is buried in so many of the products we consume outside our home (such as in a restaurant or at the potluck at church) that we would season our food with something else. American diets are so excessively high in sodium that even eliminating added salt at mealtimes does not insure acceptable levels of sodium in our diet. High blood pressure, which is negatively affected by excessive salt intake, can lead to bigger problems such as heart attacks. Given my husband's family history, we are opting to reduce our salt intake. It is interesting to note that our children don't even know that people salt their food. We just don't do it at our house. We use pepper, and everyone is happy. Using herbs in cooking enhances the flavor of food and reduces the need to season with salt.

Cutting down on white refined sugar has been an interesting journey for us. There are so many alternatives that we never even knew about. Right now we are experimenting with Sucanat, which is a pure dehydrated sugar cane juice. It is an unrefined sweetener that contains trace elements, vitamins, and minerals. The taste is similar to molasses, and it works well with whole wheat flour. It can be substituted for white or brown sugar. We put pure maple syrup on our pancakes and use it to sweeten our apple crisp. Pure maple syrup is also a good alternative to brown sugar on hot cereals. Probably the most popular sweetener at our house is honey. We purchased the largest container available at our local wholesale club until one day my husband decided to become a beekeeper.

It isn't easy to find a place to keep seven beehives in the suburbs, but it can be done. We have just completed our third season with bees and have all been learning much in the process. I appreciate the bulk supply of honey that we have on hand. Our honey is raw and unpasteurized, which is better for you than honey that has been processed with heat. It also helps us deal with local allergens. All of these refined sugar alternatives should be used in moderation.

Caffeine is something we have tried to eliminate from our home. Although it creeps into our diet when we are out, we do not purchase caffeinated beverages, coffee, or tea for our home. We do still see it come in the front door in the form of chocolate that we receive from others. While some claim that a little caffeine each day will not hurt you, I prefer to eliminate it altogether. Caffeine consumption is a habit I prefer that my children never develop.

Caffeine is present in coffee beans as well as teas, cacao seeds (cocoa and chocolate are made from these), and cola nuts (these are used to make some soft drinks). In addition to being a carcinogen, caffeine is a teratogen (a cause of birth defects). Although the studies that have been done used animals, I prefer to minimize any risk to a baby developing within me. I would rather consume beverages that are good for me and that do not raise questions of safety.

Although decaffeinated coffee may seem like a good alternative, it has its drawbacks too. The decaffeinating process uses a chemical, methylene chloride, which has caused cancer in animal studies. Another way to decaffeinate coffee is the swiss water process method. This process does not use chemicals and is preferred. Bulk coffee bins will show on the label whether it has been made using the swiss water process method. Even at this, unless it is organic, there is the issue of pesticide residue on the coffee beans. Because I drink decaf on an occasional basis, I have decided to purchase organic decaf that has been processed with the swiss water process method.

If you are thinking that maybe you should switch to tea, be careful. Teas have caffeine and tannin (tannic acid). Tannin is a suspected human carcinogen (isn't everything?). If you must drink regular tea, drink it with milk, which will bind the tannin and make it insoluble. I have found that herbal teas are the best alternative to coffee for me. There are many to choose from, and they are readily available at the grocery store. Celestial Seasonings makes a wide variety of herbal teas. They also make a tea called "Iced Delight" that we enjoy year-round. You simply fill a pitcher with water, drop in the tea bags (I use two per gallon), and put it in the refrigerator to brew. My children are beginning to enjoy this, and I feel this is a better alternative than juices, which are high in sugar. We are beginning to grow herbs such as mint that make wonderful teas. Other herbs we purchase from a food co-op. Raspberry leaves make a good medicinal tea for pregnant and nursing mothers. Echinacea is another excellent tea with medicinal value. It helps to strengthen the immune system and has been very effective for us in fighting colds and other upper respiratory infections.

While on the topic of beverages, this chapter would not be complete without a comment on milk. This may be the most controversial subject I have discussed so far. Most of us were raised with the understanding that three to four glasses of milk a day are necessary to build strong bones and teeth. I thought this was the only way to get calcium and so have been drinking three to four glasses a day for most of my life. A few years ago I was motivated by a medical problem in our family (childhood ear infections) to review my understanding of milk's role in our diet. Although we found no evidence of milk allergy with regard to our ear infection issue, my research was alarming. Milk is not necessarily the healthiest beverage we can consume.

After much study I have come to several conclusions. There are many contraindications to milk from a perspective of health. In a discussion I had with one of our health professionals, I learned that even though we consume more milk in the United States than just about anywhere else, we have one of the highest incidences of osteoporosis (a disease that is the result of bone loss—the remaining bone becomes weak and brittle). I found this troubling and set out to understand why. Here are my findings.

Although milk contains a significant amount of calcium, there are factors that prevent the body from absorbing this calcium. Protein blocks calcium absorption. If you look on the side of your milk container, you will see that milk itself contains a significant amount of protein. If you drink milk at a meal where you eat meat, the protein in the meat further blocks the absorption of calcium. There is another problem with absorption. "First of all, the calcium in cow's milk is much coarser than in human's milk and is tied up with the casein. This prevents the calcium from being absorbable. Second, most milk-drinkers and cheese-eaters consume pasteurized, homogenized, or otherwise processed products. This processing degrades the calcium, making it difficult to utilize."[17]

I have found this information in so many sources that I am concluding that if our family consumes milk at all, it will not be our major source of calcium. There are many food sources of calcium. This is a partial listing of those with the most calcium per serving: yogurt, bok choy (Chinese cabbage), broccoli, brussels sprouts, cabbage, carrots, collard greens, kale, kelp, spinach, turnip greens, blackstrap molasses, maple syrup, oats, carob, and almonds. This list is not exhaustive, nor is it prioritized in any way. I just wanted to show you the many other sources of calcium. I find the widespread debate regarding calcium supplements confusing. I try to get most of my calcium from our food and use supplements sparingly.

Another concern for milk drinkers is the bovine growth hormone, BST (Bovine Somatatropin). A few years ago our government gave the okay for farmers to use a synthetic growth hormone to stimulate greater milk production in their cows. The sad truth is that our country was already producing more milk than we were consuming. Some are concerned that the use of this hormone will lead to increased incidence of mastitis among the cows. Antibiotics are given to clear up mastitis. These antibiotics find their way into the milk and into our tummies. I now purchase our milk from a local dairy that certifies that the bovine growth hormone is not being used on their cows. We still drink some milk, but we do so in moderation. It is interesting to note that our state will not allow the dairy to advertise its milk as being free from the hormone. Is it because that might encourage others who are uninformed about the bovine growth hormone to question its use? It does make one wonder.

I encourage you to further examine the areas I have introduced. It is not my intention to make you feel that all your food is unfit for human consumption. My goal is to encourage you to ask more questions and get more answers about what you feed to your family. We as moms are responsible to know how to best take care of our families. Much information that we read about food is controversial and contradictory. Even if we are not in a position to draw specific conclusions, we can cut down our intake of questionable foods and beverages. In my family we blow it in the diet department every now and then, but overall we are committed to eating a healthy diet.

Physical health combined with spiritual and emotional health is an excellent approach to chronic wellness for your family. I have introduced many areas of potential change in food preparation and selection. Let's explore these further in the next chapter.

3

Food

I ENJOY FEELING HEALTHY, BUT HEALTH DOESN'T JUST HAPPEN. The foods we eat or do not eat have a profound effect on our health. This is true whether we are feeling well or not. Degenerative disease starts in your body long before you ever feel it. It is unwise to assume that an absence of symptoms means you are healthy. If you keep writing checks after the money is gone in your checking account, you are in trouble. The same is true for your body. If you keep consuming foods that are bad for your health, a day will come when you will be in trouble. I prefer to do all I can to eat properly while I am young, so I will still enjoy my health while I am enjoying my grandchildren and great-grandchildren. I also want to train my children to eat properly so they can enjoy health throughout their lives.

Knowing what to eat and being able to prepare and serve it are not the same thing. Although I have known about different foods for years, I still don't know how to prepare them. I have been getting familiar with foods one at a time so I am not overwhelmed. If healthy eating is a new concept to you, it will be well worth your time to make your changes slowly. I know that I am encouraged each time I master a new food, which keeps me going on to the next. My study of food seems to go in spurts. In our family we make a few changes and get used to them before I start studying again. This is a less frustrating process for me and also for my family, who must adjust their taste buds to the changes.

This chapter will contain more changes than you will probably want to attempt at one time. Remember your own unique family needs, and focus on what is important for you first. There are some foods that we eat, such as turkey and chicken and dairy products, that you may want to eliminate from your diet. We may do this ourselves in the future. We are all in different places regarding our diets. Don't get discouraged if you find that you have a lot to change. We are still in process ourselves and are always learning new things. Keeping our minds open to learning is the key to success in the food department.

Cookbooks have been invaluable to me as I have been learning about new foods and how to prepare them. I have included a listing of good cookbooks in the Resources section at the end of this book. I also have two cookbooks of my own that I have made. I use a three-ring binder for each one. (My cookbook is expanding to three volumes this summer.) My main cookbook is separated into categories such as salads, vegetables, or grains. I use clear sheet protectors to hold recipes and other information. I put anything that will help me in food preparation into this cookbook.

Good information comes from many sources, and I prefer to compile it in one place for easy access. In addition to recipes, I have a chart that lists cooking times for beans, detailed information about various grains, and other pertinent items. I have copied recipes from the library or taken them from magazines such as *Taste of Home*. I copy popular recipes from cookbooks I own and put them in my personal cookbook to make things easier. My older girls have both begun their own cookbooks in binders that they will take to their own homes in the future. My second cookbook is a collection of recipes for once-a-month cooking. More on this later.

The type of cookbooks you select must support your desire to cook healthy food for your family. I am going through my cookbooks and getting rid of most of them because they contain so many unhealthy ingredients. While it is rather simple to make ingredient substitutions, it becomes tedious when you have to substitute for most of the ingredients. There are so many good cookbooks available that we don't have to settle for recipes that are not healthy. Even in the best cookbooks, you will find that you desire to change the ingredients a little. This approach makes the recipes more useful to you.

Cooking from scratch has solved many problems that we observed in our diet. In order to eliminate artificial ingredients in our food, we had to get away from packaged foods found at the grocery store. Health food stores and food co-ops do have packaged mixes that do not have artificial ingredients, but the price of these items makes cooking from scratch a better option. I like to cook, but my goal at this time is not to spend more time in the kitchen. We now make up our own mixes or purchase a seasoning mix that is already prepared. Instead of buying a taco seasoning packet at the store, I have a Mexican seasoning mix that is available from Frontier Cooperative Herbs (800-717-HERB). Many food co-ops carry this brand. The ingredients in this Mexican seasoning are all natural and store well in a quart-sized canning jar. I use it in a variety of dishes, including beans and rice and tacos. You can make up your own seasoning blends easily. I have a jar that is an Italian blend made up of rosemary, sage, parsley, thyme, and marjoram in equal portions. I use this in Italian dishes such as lasagna and spaghetti, as well as in bean soup. It is good to stop using seasoning packets from the store and learn to season foods yourself with herbs and spices.

A great time-saver for our family is our pre-blended pancake mix. My recipe was taken from *American Wholefoods Cuisine* by David and Nikki Goldbeck, but there are mixes in other cookbooks too. This particular mix has directions for pancakes, muffins, and biscuits, which makes it versatile as well as convenient. I make the mix from freshly milled flour, which makes the nutritional value of the mix better than anything you can buy in a store. As soon as I make it, I store it in my freezer.

As you can see, I still have mixes and seasonings available. They are not filled with artificial ingredients. They are made from healthy, natural ingredients. There are recipes for homemade cookie mixes too. I have stayed away from these because I am trying to minimize sweets for desserts. A book I have found helpful in this area is *Sweet and Natural—Desserts Without Sugar, Honey, Molasses or Artificial Sweeteners* by Janet Warrington. This cookbook is easy to use and filled with some very healthy dessert alternatives.

Though cooking from scratch sounds like too much work, in reality it is as easy as the so-called "convenience" foods. I have developed a repertoire of what I call "convenience foods from scratch" for each meal of the day. We often eat oatmeal for breakfast. I buy rolled oats by the fifty-pound bag, which usually lasts us a year. This wholesome whole grain cooks up with a minimal amount of effort and a maximum amount of nutrition. Oatmeal can be put in the crock pot at night so that breakfast is waiting in the morning. Grease the inside of the crock pot, and add two cups of water for every one cup of oats. Turn on low, and cook all night (eight to nine hours). Spelt, buckwheat, and other grains also can be cooked as a hot breakfast cereal. Homemade bread toasted and served with unsweetened applesauce makes a good breakfast too. Homemade granola is another popular breakfast food. My friend, Annette, developed the following recipe to feed her growing family.

ANNETTE'S GRANOLA

12	cups oats
2/3	cup oil

* mix the next three ingredients together

    1/3   cup honey
      1   cup brown sugar**
      1   cup warm water
      2   Tbsp. vanilla
      2   cups nuts
      1   box crisp rice cereal
      1   small bag of coconut
          (add after 15 minutes of cooking)

** I eliminate the brown sugar and use a total of 1/2 cup honey.

Mix all of the ingredients (except the coconut) and bake on cookie sheets at 350 for approximately 20 minutes. Stir the mixture halfway through the baking time. (You can fit this quantity into three 13 x 9″ pans but will need to increase the cooking time to 30-40 minutes. Add the coconut after approximately 25 minutes.)

Homemade bread serves us well at lunch or when we are out of the home during a meal. If I know we will be away from home at mealtime, I just throw a loaf or two of bread in a square laundry basket along with the bread knife, jelly, dry fruit, and nuts. We bring along a gallon of pure water and some cups and can thus eat well while on the road. When we are at home, we often have homemade soup with the homemade bread. I make large stock pots of soup and freeze the leftovers. This way I make soup occasionally and usually have a good selection of soups in my freezer. Homemade soups are healthy and inexpensive compared to canned soups, which are high in salt. I don't add salt to soups, preferring spices and vegetable broth powder for flavoring.

Another lunch favorite is quesadillas. We like Mexican food

at our house. Quesadillas are simply flour tortillas filled with cheese and cooked much like you would cook grilled cheese sandwiches. Tortillas purchased at the store can have undesirable ingredients, so we are currently looking for masa harina to make our own. This can usually be found in a Mexican food store.

We have two dinner favorites that are quick and easy. Any type of pasta with tomato sauce goes over well with children. We have tomato sauce on hand that we have canned. We recently switched to whole wheat pasta, and all the children loved it. Jim wasn't so thrilled. We make fettucine alfredo once in a while when we are in a hurry. We make our own sauce. Even though it is made with milk, eggs, and butter, the fat content is not a problem for us since we have a low-fat diet.

By using your freezer you can always have a supply of healthy meal components on hand. I make bread once a week and store most of it in the freezer. Once in a while I will cook a large batch of muffins and package them in freezer bags in meal-sized portions. I usually have at least four or five main meals in the freezer, so I can pull out an entire healthy meal in the morning to serve for dinner that evening with a minimum amount of effort. I call that convenient!

Making my own bread at home is pretty easy too. At first I felt overwhelmed at the thought of it because I didn't know what I was doing. I do not use a bread machine because they only make one loaf and do not make the quality bread I desire. We use a Magic Mill DLX Kitchen Machine to knead our bread. I can make six loaves of bread at one time. When I first started making bread, I used our Kitchen Aid mixer, which can handle two loaves. I make whole grain breads from flour that I mill myself and spend less than one hour from milling to the oven. During the time the bread is being kneaded by the mixer (six minutes for freshly milled flour), I do other things in my kitchen. When the machine is through kneading the dough, I divide the dough into equal portions using a kitchen scale. I have never been able to get the same size loaves any other way. The loaves are placed in a warm oven to rise (approximately thirty minutes) and then baked for twenty-five minutes. That's it! I know I make it sound simple. That's because it *is* simple and worth a try.

A resource I found very helpful when I first started baking bread is the expertise of Marilyn Moll, who has a home business called The Urban Homemaker. She has a catalog that contains many of the supplies you will need for quantity cooking, bread making, food storage, and much more. She carries a number of very good books that are hard to find elsewhere. She is available at 800-55-BREAD for orders and 303-750-7230 for inquiries. Call for a free catalog of her products. The bread recipe that I use is the one I found in her catalog. I am including it here in proportions suitable to a Kitchen Aid mixer or a larger mixer such as my Magic Mill DLX mixer.

MARILYN'S FAMOUS WHOLE WHEAT BREAD

Kitchen Aid Mixer

1/3	cup honey
1/3	cup oil (I omit this without any problem.)
2 1/2	cups warm water (approx. 110 degrees as tested with a candy thermometer)
1 1/2	Tbsp. Saf Instant Yeast (use 2 Tbsp. of other brands of yeast)
2 1/2	tsp. salt
6-7	cups fresh whole wheat flour
1 1/2	Tbsp. dough enhancer

Combine the warm water, yeast, and 2 cups of fresh whole wheat flour in the mixing bowl. Allow to sponge for 15 minutes. Add the honey, oil, dough enhancer, salt, and 4-5 cups additional flour until the dough begins to clean the sides of the mixing bowl. (Use the dough hook.)

Set a timer for 6 minutes (for freshly milled flour) and

let your Kitchen Aid do the kneading. When the timer beeps, form two loaves of bread. Allow to rise in a slightly warmed oven (turn the oven on at 200 degrees F for five minutes, then turn off) or other warm place until doubled in size (about 30-60 minutes).

Bake loaves for 25-30 minutes in a 350 degree F oven. Bread is cooked through when it sounds hollow when tapped on the bottom and when the top and sides are a golden brown color.

Larger Mixer Method

2/3	cup honey
2/3	cup oil (you can omit this)
6	cups warm water (approx. 110 degree reading on a candy thermometer)
3	Tbsp. Saf Instant Yeast (use 4 Tbsp. of other brands of yeast)
1 1/2	Tbsp. salt
16-20	cups fresh whole wheat flour
3	Tbsp. dough enhancer

Combine 2 cups of the warm water, yeast, and 2 cups of fresh whole wheat flour in the mixing bowl. Allow to sponge for 15 minutes. Add the rest of the water, honey, oil, dough enhancer, and salt and 14-18 cups additional flour until the dough begins to clean the sides of the mixing bowl.

Set the timer on the mixer for 6 minutes (for freshly milled flour) at the medium speed. When the machine is done kneading, divide the dough into five or six loaves. Allow to rise in a slightly warmed oven (turn the oven on at 200 degrees F for five minutes, then turn off) or other warm place until doubled in size (about 30-60 minutes).

Bake loaves for 25-30 minutes in a 350 degree F oven. Bread is cooked through when it sounds hollow when tapped on the bottom and when the top and sides are a golden brown color.

Quantity Cooking

In recent years the concept of cooking thirty meals all at once on one day has gained popularity. It makes much sense to maximize your time and your productivity by cutting all the vegetables at once and reusing pots and pans without washing and putting away between each use. As I mentioned, I have my own personal cookbook of recipes that I use when I cook in quantity.

In my family, my husband does not like to eat a meal from the freezer every night. We have some meals from the freezer and others that are cooked the day we eat them. When I prepare meals for the freezer, I usually make enough for fifteen meals. A friend of mine who recently went back to work full-time makes her meals for the week on the weekend and then freezes them. Regardless of your preference of how many meals to make at a time, there are good books that show you how to tackle this project. A comprehensive guide that tells you exactly what to do is found in *Dinner's in the Freezer!* by Jill Bond. This book answers many questions about quantity cooking for the freezer. It includes recipes, charts, resources, and much practical information. If you prefer a vegetarian diet, *Cooking What Comes Naturally—A Month's Worth of Practical Vegetarian Menus* by Nikki Goldbeck contains complete menus for a month. It is not oriented toward putting meals in the freezer but is very useful in planning ahead for the month.

My own system for cooking in quantity varies with our family circumstances. During pregnancy I like to have enough on hand in the freezer to carry us through days or weeks where I don't feel like cooking. I don't prefer to set aside an entire day for cooking freezer meals, so I use a system that I call "incidental preparedness." When I cook something like lasagna or a casserole, I usually make enough to freeze one meal. Over time the selection and quantity of freezer meals grows without any major effort on my part. It is just as easy to make a double recipe as it is to make a single recipe.

Another way that I am prepared is by having planned leftovers. On days when we have piano lessons or are out of the home in the afternoon, I plan to have leftovers. Since I plan my menus a week at a time, it is easy to see when to schedule leftovers. It is also a time-saver to use ingredients from one meal to make the meal the next day. Rice is easy to cook in a large quantity. It may accompany chicken on Monday and then show up in a casserole on Tuesday. Don't forget about your crock pot. It is a lifesaver when you know you will be away from home during the day. It is very pleasant to come home at the end of a busy day to smell dinner cooking itself. Working mothers can benefit from using the crock pot often.

Sometimes I cook in bulk if there is a good sale. If chicken legs are a good price, I can cook up a large quantity in a stock pot. I then make chicken noodle soup. I cube up the chicken after taking it off the bones and package it in meal-sized portions to go in the freezer. I don't do this often because we don't eat a lot of meat. The meat I freeze lasts us a long time, and we then have a good supply of chicken noodle soup too.

Depending upon the size of your family, you can prepare meals ahead of time and store them in the freezer portion of your refrigerator. For most of us, it is prudent to invest in a large freezer. It will not only provide space for freezer meals but will also allow you to freeze vegetables and fruits when they are in season and at a good price. Once you have a freezer, be sure to keep a list of freezer meals on the door so you know what is in there without having to open the door.

Menu planning has helped me consistently serve healthy food to my family. I used to decide what to cook each day, but weekly menu planning is much more efficient. Some women plan a month at a time. I find that with our changing schedule, a week of menus fits our family's needs. It helps me to know what I am serving at each meal of the day so I can be prepared. If I am serving a hot cereal in the morning, I may choose to measure the grain the night before so I only need to add water in the morning. Underneath each item on my menu I mark "freezer" if I am planning on using something in the freezer. That way I can know at a glance what needs to be taken out to defrost for all of the meals for that day. I like to take a look at the dinner menu around lunchtime so I can make a portion of it ahead of time. I usually will try to make the salad right after lunch since cutting up the vegetables can be time-consuming.

I hope you can see that by taking a little time to get organized, you can successfully cook food from scratch without spending long hours in the kitchen. The time spent is well worth it when you consider the free time you will have because you will not be ill so often due to a poor diet. I encourage you to read the testimonies of two women who were very ill and made a complete turnaround of their conditions through proper diet and nutrition. Their stories compel me to keep improving our diet even when I don't feel like it. I've already mentioned *Healthy Habits—20 Simple Ways to Improve Your Health* by David and Anne Frahm.

Health Begins in Him—Biblical Steps to Optimal Health and Nutrition by Terry Dorian is one of the most encouraging books I have read about getting serious about proper nutrition. Her personal testimonies of her own journey to optimal health lends perspective on how far all of us can progress when we commit to making the necessary dietary changes. *The Cookbook, Health Begins in Him* is a follow-up book that is must reading for those who want to do it right.

If you are going to cook in quantity using quality ingredients, you need to know where to purchase these at the best price. Price and quality go hand in hand, and only you can decide for yourself which products are worth the extra price. We often buy our milk from a local dairy that verifies that the milk is free from bovine growth hormones. It is more expensive than milk in the store, but we feel the price is worth it. We only use about one gallon per week for seven people.

Organic grain is not much more expensive than non-organic, so we opt for organic grain. We have found a source for organic raw milk cheese that is very reasonable (Morningland Dairy, 6248 Co. Road 2980, Mountain View, MO 65548; phone: 417-469-3817). They deliver UPS, and since we buy in bulk it is very convenient for us. Organic produce in our area is prohibitively expensive for our family, so most of the time we do not purchase it. In the summer we have our own garden, the best source of all for organic produce. We do purchase some of our produce from the local farmer's market in the summer where I can pay a wholesale price for produce I buy in quantity.

Food co-ops are valuable opportunities for purchasing healthy foods at reasonable prices. You will notice that health food stores charge prices that are outside the budgets of most of us. These same foods can be purchased from a food co-op at a much lower price. Here is a listing of some possibilities:

NORTHEASTERN UNITED STATES

Northeast Co-Op
P.O. Box 8188
Brattleboro, VT 05304
802-257-5856

Dutch Valley Bulk Food Distributors
Meyerstown, PA 17067
800-733-4191

Crusoe Island Natural and Organic Groceries
267 Route 89 S.
Savannah, NY 13146
315-365-2816

Federation of Ohio River Cooperatives (FORC)
320 Outerbelt Street, Suite E
Columbus, OH 43213
614-861-2446

Associated Buyers
P.O. Box 399
Barrington, NH 03825
603-664-5656

SERVING TX, LA, OK, MS, MO, AR, KS, AL, GA, TN, FL

Ozark Co-Op Warehouse
Box 1528
Fayetteville, AR 72702
501-521-4920

SERVING AZ, NM, PARTS OF TX, CO, UT, NV, CA

Tucson Cooperative Warehouse
350 South Toole Avenue
Tucson, AZ 85701
520-884-9951

SERVING AZ, CA, ID, MT, NV, NM, OR, UT, WA

Mountain Peoples Warehouse
12745 Earhart Avenue
Auburn, CA 95602
916-889-9531

SERVING WA, OR, SOME OF CANADA, ID, MT, AK

Mountain Peoples Warehouse Northwest
4005 6th Avenue S.
Seattle, WA 98108
800-336-8872

SERVING ME, VT, NH, MA, CT, NY, SC, NC, VA, GA, FL, PARTS OF PA, MD, DE, WV, AL, TN, KY

United Natural Foods
260 Lake Road
Dayville, CT 06241
860-779-2800

SERVING IA, IL, IN, KS, MI, MN, MO, NE, SD, WI, WY

Blooming Prairie Warehouse, Inc.
2340 Heinz Road
Iowa City, IA 52240
319-337-6448

SERVING WI, IL, IN, MI, MN, ND, SD, PARTS OF MT, OH

North Farm
204 Regas Road
Madison, WI 53714
608-241-2667

SERVING WA, OR, ID, MT, PART OF ND

Azure Standard
79709 Dufur Valley Road
Dufur, OR 97021
541-467-2230

Walton Feed, Inc.
135 North 10th
P.O. Box 307
Montpelier, ID 83254
800-847-0465

Frontier Cooperative Herbs
Box 299

Norway, IA 52318
319-227-7991

These addresses represent the suppliers of food and other items. They should be able to give you the name of the nearest group of people who receive deliveries from their warehouse. A typical food co-op has a job for each member to perform. The time commitment may be as little as an hour or two each month to several hours. I have tried a number of arrangements and have found that I do not have time to commit to a job in a food co-op.

In the Chicagoland area I have come up with an alternative that I can do on my own. I schedule my order at my own convenience and order as often or as seldom as I want. If you live near a large city, by doing some research you may be able to come up with similar arrangements.

I order from Country Life Natural Foods in Pullman, MI (616-236-5011). For an order of $250 or more, a truck will deliver my food to my door with no delivery fee. Minimum orders of $200 incur a $10 delivery fee. These fees are for delivery to my area. They are a parent company to some smaller distributors,. primarily in the Midwest. They are a good place to get started without joining a food co-op.

Cooking in quantity and buying food in bulk has greatly simplified the business of eating well at our house. The time and money saved coupled with the healthier food we are eating has been a tremendous blessing to our family. By taking advantage of produce in season and preserving it, we have stretched both our money and our time. While the investment of time and energy during canning is great, we have this food readily available for an entire year! Let's explore canning and freezing and see how this can further simplify your meal preparation.

Some of you probably don't even know what I mean by canning. It is becoming a lost art in our culture. Many of our grandmothers or great-grandmothers spent long days during harvest canning the produce from the garden. Peaches, green beans, applesauce, and tomato sauce are some popular items for canning. We began our first year of canning with just applesauce. Using our Kitchen Aid mixer and an attachment, we included our children in the process. All of our apples were free since they came off our tree or other people's trees that we are allowed to pick. Each year we seem to add more variety to our growing repertoire of canned foods. We make at least one trip a year to Michigan to pick peaches. We have a location in Illinois where we pick blueberries (we freeze them). Last year we picked a couple of bushels of apples in Wisconsin.

The best way for you to learn to can is to use the same method we did. We bought a water bath canner (garage sale) and some jars. We purchased a copy of the *Ball Blue Book—Guide to Home Canning, Freezing and Dehydration* and read the directions. (You can order this by calling the Ball Corporation at 800-859-2255.) And off we went. I will add at this point that my husband is an integral part of this process. This is the fifth year that we will be canning, and three of those five years I have been in the last trimester of a pregnancy. I so enjoy having the food that we preserve available throughout the year, I can't remember how I managed without it.

Some of our fruits and vegetables we prefer to freeze. Frozen fruit makes a breakfast drink without much preparation. Sue Gregg's breakfast cookbook explains in detail how to make these healthy breakfast shakes. Vegetables must be blanched (cooked briefly in boiling water and then cooled) before they are frozen. Instructions for how long to cook different foods came with my blancher.

By now you are probably wondering what new kitchen items you will need to cook in the manner I have described. The next chapter will help you know what you need and why. Happy cooking!

4

Equipment

IN TRANSFORMING YOUR EATING REGIME FROM FAST FOOD AND prepackaged mixes to healthy meals cooked from scratch, you may find there are certain items you need that are not currently a part of your kitchen. It is ironic that as we filled out our wish lists for bridal showers and wedding gifts, we did not have knowledge of what we really needed in our kitchens. We may need to get rid of useless gadgets and equipment to make room for the new. For the purpose of this chapter, I will define equipment as anything you use in the preparation or storage of food. Much of the time it is not necessary to buy the best. Determine what is adequate for your own needs, and buy those items as finances allow. If you need many things, consider having a garage sale or some other creative fund-raising event to give you the money you need to equip yourself for better and more economical eating. If you go out to eat regularly, consider stopping this and set aside the money you save to use for equipment. You know best how to raise money in your own household.

There are many kitchen gadgets on the market today. Some popular items for the kitchen are a poor buy, while other beneficial equipment is hardly known by most homemakers. It is my purpose to explore both of these areas At the outset we need to understand what the purpose of equipment is in our homes. First, we want to streamline our tasks whenever we can. A simple purchase of some kitchen shears was a big help to me in dealing with chicken. I have found other uses for the shears too. We should consider equipment that will facilitate optimal results. Although I know how to make bread by hand, I find it easier and much quicker to use a machine to knead the dough (not a bread machine—more on this later). Finally, we need to use equipment that will provide safe storage for our bulk food purchases. Plastic buckets that are used for frosting by bakeries have been useful in the storage of various grains at our home. A chain grocery store in our area gives them away free from their bakery. The lids shut tightly, and we purchased a tool from a restaurant supplier to open them. Other possibilities for locating these buckets are Dairy Queens and local bakeries. There are two sizes. The largest holds about twenty-five pounds of grain. We have used the smaller size for storing honey and for other assorted uses.

As I list what I consider to be basic kitchen utensils, bear in mind that this list is not exhaustive. Different cooks prefer different equipment in their kitchen. My goal is to give those who have not done much cooking some idea of what they need. I also want to help experienced cooks who want to cook in quantity to know what additions to their kitchen will make quantity cooking run smoothly.

Probably my most practical wedding gift was our Chicago cutlery knife set. We have added to the set over the years, and thanks to proper upkeep (sharpening and keeping the wooden handles from soaking in the sink) they are still serving us well. We use our bread knife and vegetable chopper almost daily. These knives are costly, but we buy them for at least half off when they go on sale at a local department store. Farm and Fleet stores carry this brand too. These are a lasting investment since you only have to buy them once.

I consider a good cutting board essential. Two or three are advisable to facilitate multiple tasks performed simultaneously in the kitchen. I had plastic cutting boards for a time, but I have since learned that wood boards are better for a couple of reasons. Wood is better for sanitation because the wood draws moisture out of the germs so they die; germs live more comfortably on plastic cutting boards. Wood is also easier on the knives, so they won't dull as quickly.

Multiple sets of measuring cups and spoons help speed up the cooking process. I have two two-cup glass measuring cups and a four-cup glass measuring cup for liquids. We have two or three sets of plastic dry measuring cups and three sets of measuring spoons. These can be found at garage sales and eliminate the need to keep washing things out after measuring different ingredients. If I want my daughters to work alongside me in the kitchen, I need to have enough tools for us to work together. It is good to have a number of wooden spoons on hand as well.

Canisters with tightly fitting lids are needed to store homemade mixes and items you purchase in bulk. Bulk items often are packaged in bags that are not good for storage once they are opened. Tupperware makes a canister set that is plastic and works well in the freezer. I store my homemade pancake mix in one of these. Quart or pint canning jars serve a storage purpose too, if you are careful to keep them out of the light. Since I have learned that so many things are sensitive to light, I store most everything inside a cabinet where it is dark. Canning jars are perfect to hold seasoning mixes that you make yourself or buy in bulk.

Beyond a good set of pots and pans, I like to have a crock pot. This sure comes in handy when you are not available to cook. Sometimes I will put the meal in the night before and set it in the refrigerator. In the morning I take it out and turn it on. By dinnertime the meal is done, and I did not have to do anything that day. A large stock pot is a good addition to your pots and pans too. Even smaller families can use a large pot to cook spaghetti sauce, soup, or something else in quantity so there will be leftovers to freeze.

If you want to cook a large quantity of food, make sure you have enough pots and pans, cookie sheets, muffin tins, and bread pans. If you mix batter for six dozen muffins, it helps to have at least four muffin tins so you don't have to wait for the first batch to cool before putting the second batch in the oven. I have extra 13 x 9" Pyrex glass cooking dishes with lids to fill with meals I double for the freezer. If you do not have the plastic lids, Ziploc makes a jumbo freezer bag that will fit a 13 x 9" pan. I have found these at Wal-Mart. I store many freezer meals in freezer bags, but certain items such as lasagna and some casseroles work better in the dish they will be baked in. I have an abundance of plastic containers in which I can place freezer meals or leftovers. I try to minimize the use of plastic bags whenever I can and reuse my own containers.

Last, but not least, is my kitchen timer. I have one that will let me time three different things at once. The truth is, I use timers so often that I wear them out. Once your food is in the oven or your bread is rising, you can go elsewhere in your house or go outside. As long as the timer is there to call you, there is no need to stay in the kitchen. I set my timer for a few minutes before the item should be done so I can take it out sooner if it is cooking faster than I thought it would.

The workhorse of my kitchen is truly my Kitchen Aid mixer. Over a decade ago my husband suggested getting one. At the time I had no idea why I needed it. For more information on this mixer and other stand mixers, see *Consumer Reports*, November 1994. Initially I used the Kitchen Aid to make bread using the dough hook. You can make two loaves at a time with this machine. We use attachments to the Kitchen Aid for processing fruits and vegetables for canning. There are a couple of different models of this mixer, and they are often on sale. My daughters operate this machine with ease, which makes it the perfect mixer for my kitchen.

I have had a larger mixer as well for the past couple of years. I purchased a larger mixer primarily to use for mixing bread. It will knead enough dough to make five to six loaves of bread. I now make bread just once a week. If you are interested in bread making, I suggest that you consider a Kitchen Aid mixer or a larger mixer (see Terry Dorian's "Green Pastures—The New Resource Guide," 800-295-3477 or Marilyn Moll's "The Urban Homemaker" catalog, 800-55-BREAD). We have an electric grain mill so we can mill our own grain, which is by far the healthiest alternative. I purchased a candy thermometer to test the temperature of the water so I don't ruin the yeast. This is not essential, but it makes me comfortable to know that the water is not too hot. A few months ago I purchased a kitchen scale to weigh my bread dough. I had trouble dividing the dough evenly so the loaves are the same size. The scale solves this problem and offers other uses too.

If you are considering purchasing a bread machine, I would recommend that you consider the Kitchen Aid or a larger mixer. A bread machine only makes one loaf of bread at a time and is using your electricity for hours on end. I have not seen the quality of bread from a bread machine to be any better than bread mixed by a mixer and then baked in the oven. On the contrary, I have eaten bread from a bread machine that was not completely cooked on the inside and overall was of poor quality. I don't really see that they save time either. I can grind my wheat and have my bread in the oven (five to six loaves) in forty-five minutes. If you own a bread machine and are happy with it, by all means use it. If you own one that just sits on the counter, then think about selling it and buying a bread mixer instead.

If you are ready to begin canning, there are a number of items you will need. Quart and pint canning jars are often available at no cost if you let people know you need them. Elderly ladies still have canning supplies, and as they pass away, there is usually nobody who wants the supplies. We currently have over sixty dozen jars. Many of them were gladly given to us because the people were happy that we would be using them. Along with the jars you will need rings and seals. These can be found at Wal-Mart.

Other helpful items include tongs to lift the jars out of the water (we have more than one), a metal wand to lift the seals out of the water, and a gadget that strips the corn off of the cob. These are available at Wal-Mart, or you can request a catalog from the Ball Corporation by calling 800-859-2255. I recommend this free catalog because it has pictures and will help you see what you need, particularly when you are getting started.

We have both a water bath canner and a pressure canner. We use the water bath canner to process applesauce and tomato sauce, which are the main focus of our canning efforts. Last year we processed green beans in the pressure canner with excellent results. The best resource for specifics regarding canning is the *Ball Blue Book—Guide to Home Canning, Freezing and Dehydration.* I have seen these at Wal-Mart during the harvest season, or you may contact Ball directly at 800-859-2255. Water bath canners are as easy to find in our area as canning jars. I have purchased at least half a dozen for two to three dollars apiece at garage sales. We own a blancher too. This I purchased new and use frequently during harvest season. Fresh vegetables must be blanched before they are frozen. I use the blancher most often for green beans. As I expand my knowledge, I will be using it for much more. Two or three large stock pots are handy when you are processing large quantities. We can almost 100 quarts of applesauce in one day, so we need a couple of stock pots. We use them for spaghetti sauce too. Long-handled wooden spoons are necessary to stir such large quantities of sauce in large stock pots.

Our applesauce and tomato sauce processing is greatly simplified using attachments to our Kitchen Aid mixer. The investment made to purchase the attachments was well worth it. You need a couple of large bowls because the good sauce goes into one bowl and the skins, seeds, and other waste goes into a second bowl using these attachments.

After working so diligently to process your produce, make sure you have adequate storage for your frozen and canned goods. We purchased the largest upright freezer we could find during a time of tight cash flow. A freezer is an important capital investment in the food picture. We enjoy blueberries, strawberries, peaches, green beans, and more year-round because we have a freezer to store them in. I only buy these fruits and vegetables when they are at the best annual price (my harvest record helps me know when this is), and then we eat them all year long. We are able to eat better food at a lower cost than if we did not have a freezer.

Food that you can does not need to take up a lot of room. Jim built shelves specifically for our canning jars, located in our crawl space. Even if your home does not have a nice pantry area, there is *somewhere* that you can make one. A friend of mine who lives in a warm climate decided to turn her coat closet into a pantry since they didn't need to wear coats most of the year. Be creative. Every house has a spot to store your canned goods.

A piece of equipment that I use primarily during harvest season is my dehydrator. This is a good way to provide nutritious and tasty snacks for your family. I have not used mine extensively yet, but my plans include drying blueberries, strawberries, cherries, and apples to throw into homemade granola. Bananas are very simple to dry and are a big hit with the children. When bananas are on sale, you can take advantage of the price and buy extra to dehydrate.

Last summer I finally found a juicer at a garage sale. At 25 percent of its original cost, I felt it was a bargain. I am a novice juicer. My main reason for getting the juicer was to use it during the harvest season when fresh vegetables are in abundance. Only a few weeks after purchasing the machine I was ill, and Jim made me some carrot juice with garlic to help me get better. *Juicing for Life* by Cherie Calbom and Maureen Keane can help you identify what type of juice to make to help with various ailments. The opening chapter explains the benefits of juicing.

Although you don't need all of these items, depending upon what you hope to accomplish, you may want to acquire many of them. I have mentioned garage sales many times in this chapter in the hope that you will think of other alternatives besides running to the store to buy these things. Possibly by using some of my suggestions in the next chapter, you will be able to save enough money to afford some of these bigger ticket items. Read on!

5

Saving Money

AFTER GETTING YOU EXCITED ABOUT SPENDING MONEY ON NEW equipment in the last chapter, I will now want to encourage you to save money. As I have indicated previously, sometimes in order to save money, we need to spend money. How we can best spend our resources, be it time, money, or anything else, is a question of balancing many options. Often money is not the only consideration in decision-making. How can we possibly make any sense of all of our options when it comes to money?

I believe a biblical understanding of what money is and what it is not is foundational to sound decision-making regarding money.

Money Is Not a Measure of Success

I do not believe our culture knows this. The "buy more, get more, own more" philosophies of recent decades are not consistent with the teaching of Jesus. In Luke 12:15 Jesus is addressing a large gathering when He says, "Watch out! Be on your guard against all kinds of greed; a man's life does not consist in the abundance of his possessions." Money buys possessions; so in order to have more possessions, people need more money. Rather than money being a measure of success, it often breeds greed for more money. A Bible teacher said it well when he said, "The family that buys together, cries together."

Having a lot of things doesn't necessarily mean you own them either. Many people owe much more than they own. Ultimately we cannot take these things with us when we die anyway. Psalm 49 addresses this well in its consideration of money in relation to eternal life: "Do not be overawed when a man grows rich, when the splendor of his house increases; for he will take nothing with him when he dies, his splendor will not descend with him. Though while he lived he counted himself blessed—and men praise you when you prosper—he will join the generation of his fathers, who will never see the light of life" (vv. 16-19).

Personally I find that having *less* is a measure of success for our family. As we voluntarily simplify our lives by doing away with some of the conveniences we are accustomed to, we are experiencing freedom. (If we have less stuff, we need less money to live.) Most recently we decided to unplug our microwave and store it in the garage to see if we could do without it. At first I was thinking this was silly since it is so easy to use the probe to get the water just the right temperature for bread baking, heat up leftovers, melt butter, etc. Besides, we already own it! Would you believe that after only one week without my microwave I am doing fine? We have an older model that took up a lot of counter space, and I am enjoying the extra space. I have found that I really don't need the microwave at all. Some of the things I used the microwave for actually work better on the stove top or in the oven. Success does not come from having more things or having more money, but rather from maximizing what you have. Sometimes you don't even need what you have.

Money Is Not a Component of Self-worth

People with a lot of money generally get a sense of self-worth as they consider the car they drive, the clothes they wear, or the house they live in. While externally they seem to have a sense of well-being, internally, in many cases, their life is hollow and their heart heavy. On the other hand, there are those who do not have enough money and therefore believe they are of no value. They feel useless. Self-worth to a Christian is not dependent on whether a person has or does not have money. Self-worth to a Christian is based on what God thinks of us. We are His children, we are all equal before God, and we are joint-heirs with Christ. Galatians 3:26-28 says, "You are all sons of God through faith in Christ Jesus, for all of you who were baptized into Christ have clothed yourselves with Christ. There is neither Jew nor Greek, slave nor free, male nor female, for you are all one in Christ Jesus."

Financial status has no bearing on our worth to God. If it doesn't matter to Him, it shouldn't matter to us. We are God's children, and that is where we find our self-worth. "Yet to all who received him, to those who believed in his name, he gave the right to become children of God" (John 1:12).

Money Is Not a Reward for Godly Living

I don't know where the idea originated that if we do good work, are good people, and live good lives, we will get more money. Life doesn't work that way. Just a few months ago the court declared that my husband's employer did not have to disclose reasons behind their refusal to promote him to lieutenant even though he had been informed that he would be promoted. He participated in training and a work assignment related to the promotion, but they wouldn't tell him why they passed him over. This circumstance amounts to the loss of about $40,000 for our family over the years until Jim can retire. Good work does not mean that you will make more money. How many things are there in the life of a mother that money cannot buy anyway? No amount of money can buy us sleep. We cannot buy peace of mind in the midst of a hectic day. We cannot buy the love of our spouse. You see, some of the best things in life cannot be bought. They are given to us by God. These are the true riches. "In vain you rise early and stay up late, toiling for food to eat—for he grants sleep to those he loves" (Psalm 127:2).

Money Is Not a Guarantee for Contentment

Do you know someone who seems to have a need to buy something to be happy? It doesn't usually end with buying one thing. Often people will make multiple purchases of items they do not need. Shopping takes on new meaning as the person shops for the sake of shopping instead of shopping for necessary items. It doesn't matter what they buy as long as they buy *something*. This type of person will often be a collector, justifying yet one more trip to the store to buy another item. Never having enough, they need more and more to be satisfied. Seeking contentment through money or possessions is not an isolated problem for women. Many women are plagued by the results of their misdirected efforts. An excellent book offering help to such a woman is *A Woman's Place Is in the Mall and Other Lies* by Karen O'Connor. This is must reading for anyone wishing to break out of such patterns.

Paul's discussion of contentment in 1 Timothy makes no reference to having money: "But godliness with contentment is great gain. For we brought nothing into the world, and we can take nothing out of it. But if we have food and clothing, we will be content with that" (6:6-8). Contentment does not come from money. The converse is often true. "Whoever loves money never has money enough; whoever loves wealth is never satisfied with his income. This too is meaningless" (Ecclesiastes 5:10). Solomon ends his discussion on the futility of riches with a beautiful description of a person who is content: "Moreover, when God gives any man wealth and possessions, and enables him to enjoy them, to accept his lot and be happy in his work—this is a gift of God. He seldom reflects on the days of his life, because God keeps him occupied with gladness of heart" (Ecclesiastes 5:19-20).

Money Is a Test

At the beginning of Luke 16, Jesus tells a story about a man who is accused of poorly managing his rich employer's possessions. When the manager hears that the rich man no longer will allow him to manage his possessions, the manager decides to radically reduce the amount owed by the rich man's debtors. The rich man is pleased that the manager acts in a shrewd manner. The words of Jesus at the end of this story are a powerful reminder of our responsibility with money: "Whoever can be trusted with very little can also be trusted with much, and whoever is dishonest with very little will also be dishonest with much. So if you have not been trustworthy in handling worldly wealth, who will trust you with true riches? And if you have not been trustworthy with someone else's property, who will give you property of your own? No servant can serve two masters. Either he will hate the one and love the other, or he will be devoted to the one and despise the other. You cannot serve both God and Money" (vv. 10-13).

Money Is a Tool to Teach Us Things.

This principle really hits home with our family. A few years ago we were blessed with the opportunity to purchase a brand-new pop-up camper. Since we rarely buy big-ticket items new, this was truly a treat! Not long after we bought our camper, a friend of ours asked if her family could borrow it for house guests who would be staying at their home after a wedding. We were not too interested in loaning out our spotless camper since we did not know how well it would be taken care of by the guests; so we declined. This happened in the fall, and we stored the camper in our garage all that winter. In the spring my husband was setting it up to prepare for a trip to visit some friends. Imagine our surprise to find that there were rice and beans left in the camper over the winter! We'd moved and had a baby that previous summer and fall, and cleaning out the camper had been overlooked.

That in itself was not so bad had it not been for the mice. Attracted by the food, the mice found that the curtains and the canvas (made out of a new fabric called Evolution 3, which we were later told by an auto upholsterer is very tasty to mice) kept them well fed over the winter. Of the eight panels of curtains, only two were not shredded. All but one panel of the canvas had at least one hole. Our screened-in room had a big hole in the screen. And we had not even used it yet!

This type of disaster is not covered by insurance. Our new camper now had a definitive "used" look about it. Some time later my friend approached me and suggested that had we let them borrow the camper, they would have discovered the rice and beans before the mice did. My husband and I immediately realized that we had been selfishly clinging to our possessions. This was a profound reminder to us that all we have is by the grace of God, and we are to "share with God's people who are in need" (Romans 12:13). In addition, we understood in a more practical way the wisdom found in Matthew 6:19: "Do not store up for yourselves treasures on earth, where moth and rust destroy, and where thieves break in and steal."

Money Is a Testimony

Where do our priorities lie? How do we use our money? On what do we spend our money? The book of James teaches practical Christian living. In chapter 5 James issues a warning to the rich:

"Now listen, you rich people, weep and wail because of the misery that is coming upon you. Your wealth has rotted, and moths have eaten your clothes. Your gold and silver are corroded. Their corrosion will testify against you and eat your flesh like fire. You have hoarded wealth in the last days. . . . You have lived on earth in luxury and self-indulgence. You have fattened yourselves in the day of slaughter" (vv. 1-3, 5). Are we keepers? Are we savers? Or do we give what we are not using to someone who can use it? We have established a sharing table at MOPs (Mothers of Preschoolers). If you find something you want, you can simply pick it up and take it. I love to take things there because I know they will go to good use. I have also found some great things there for my own family.

Money Is Trouble!

I probably have not told you anything new. It has become a cliché in our culture that money is the root of all evil. This comes out of 1 Timothy 6:10, though it is usually slightly misquoted: "For the love of money is a root of all kinds of evil. Some people, eager for money, have wandered from the faith and pierced themselves with many griefs." Many verses in the Bible speak of the perils of money. Moses addressed this in Deuteronomy 8:13-14 as he talked to the Israelites, warning them that riches can lead to forgetting God. His words speak loudly to us today: ". . . and when your herds and flocks grow large and your silver and gold increase and all you have is multiplied, then your heart will become proud and you will forget the Lord your God, who brought you out of Egypt, out of the land of slavery." An abundance of money breeds self-reliance. I know that for our family, our faith has grown much stronger by having only enough money to make ends meet. There is little extra for emergencies or expenses beyond our budget. Yet we have found time and time again that our needs and our desires have been met.

Greed is another temptation that is a byproduct of having money, or at least of depending too much on that money. When our riches increase, we tend to want more and more. The stakes are high. as we learn from Ephesians 5:5: "For of this you can be sure: No immoral, impure or greedy person—such a man is an idolater—has any inheritance in the kingdom of Christ and of God." Peter advises elders to avoid greed and suggests an alternative: "Be shepherds of God's flock that is under your care, serving as overseers—not because you must, but because you are willing, as God wants you to be; not greedy for money, but eager to serve; not lording it over those entrusted to you, but being examples to the flock" (1 Peter 5:2-3).

Understanding biblical principles regarding money has led Jim and me to make changes in the way we view money as it relates to our family. We no longer seek increases in our income but rather strive for reductions in our budget. Many of the decisions about employment that I shared in the "Lifestyle Simplification" chapter involved reductions in our income. Circumstances originally forced us to be creative, but now we are choosing to live frugally. We value our family life highly and prioritize it ahead of gaining money. Consequently, at least so far, we have had to make do with less income for the sake of our family. This may sound like a great sacrifice, but remember that money is not the source of our happiness. Certainly the things that money can buy do not replace the cohesiveness of a family who spends time together. Further, we have found that we can still have what we want by being creative. Getting things free, at garage sales, and doing without are just some of the ways we make this work.

A number of good books offer practical money-saving tips. I have mentioned some of them in the Resources section, and it is not my desire to duplicate these. I recommend that you purchase one or two of them as reference material for saving money. What I want you to know is what we learned through our own family's downsizing experience that helped us get through the process. The tips I am sharing are more of a story about our own family's approach to making ends meet than they are a list of methods. What I am doing may not work for you, but it could get you thinking about how to make a change for your own family. This is my purpose in including this chapter.

I can't say that our family's downsizing has been totally uplifting. It has not. It took time to readjust our thinking away from being upwardly mobile in corporate America. We were raised in a generation that measured success by gross annual income. It was sheer folly to walk away from that ideal. Or was it?

Now that we are comfortably living a simpler life, I realize that I have gained far more than I have lost. Our combined income before children was higher than our current income, which supports our growing family of seven. I have traded my high heels for Reeboks, office politics for child training, and the fierce competition of coworkers for loving children. A good book that encourages this transition is *Coming Home to Raise Your Children, a Survival Guide for Moms*. Written by my friend Christine Field, a former trial lawyer, it gives you the perspective of what really matters.

Living Within Your Means

Living within our means has been challenging—circumstances do not always turn out the way we hope they will. Some of the decisions we made became pivotal to our success as our incomes decreased. Anyone can employ these same methods to suit their own family. All of us can choose to live *below* our means. Just because we expect a raise or a promotion (remember, my husband's promotion never came through—this had never happened before at his fire department) does not mean we have to upgrade cars or our house. It is prudent to see this increase in income as "money left at the end of the month." A two-income family can choose to use only one income for living expenses and save the other income. After a while it is then possible for the wife to quit working to raise and train the children. If you max out your expenses to utilize both incomes, you lose this opportunity.

Living within our means has meant paying cash for purchases. When I had the checkbook in my purse, I could always write a check, even if the money in the account was meant for something else. This led to overspending. I now have separate envelopes for the budgeted amount in each category of my responsibility. My envelopes cover food, gas, clothing, vitamins, garage sales (we budget for this), entertainment, home-school curriculum, and gifts. I get a weekly allowance and also five dollars per week for "mad money" (which most often gets spent on food). I have finite amounts of money at my disposal. If I am prudent in my spending, I have more money. I also have the freedom to "borrow" from one envelope to the next. We have one VISA card, which is used for telephone orders or emergencies. If the VISA is used, the balance is *always* paid off each month.

When my husband was laid off for a year and worked in construction, it would have been easy to use the credit card over the winter and then, when he was back at work, pay it off. We chose not to do this and believe it was a wise choice. Once you carry a balance on a credit card, it is too easy to do so every month. When you carry a balance on your card, you are essentially financing debt. Credit cards are the worst way to finance debt.

Budgeting

We use Larry Burkett's *The Financial Planning Workbook* to organize our finances. His ministry, Christian Financial Concepts, offers many good resources (800-722-1976). By itemizing our expenses, we were able to see areas where we could pull in our belts. When you break down expenses by category, it is easier to see where too much money is being spent.

Don't be intimidated by the concept of a budget. Basically you are establishing a known pattern of monthly obligations instead of running your finances by the seat of your pants. It is important to have control over your own personal finances. Once you know what your expenses are, you can better administer your income appropriately. In addition to Larry Burkett's resources, there is another book that I would recommend to someone who is feeling unsure about how to even begin to use a budget. It is called *Living Smart, Spending Less Workbook, Wise Choices That Stretch Your Income* by Stephen and Amanda Sorenson. This book uses a number of charts to help you sort out your finances. I found it easy to use and learned some things myself.

A benefit we have enjoyed while using a budget has been our ability to stay out of debt. The only money that we owe is for housing. We prepay our principal on our mortgage as often as we can and desire to be completely debt-free as soon as possible. We buy only what we have the money to pay for and do without the rest. Even emergencies such as our van catching fire were remedied without long-term debt. Money set aside for such an emergency can eliminate the need for any debt in such a circumstance. If you are in debt now and would like to live debt-free, I recommend Larry Burkett's book *Debt-Free Living—How to Get out of Debt (and Stay Out)*. In this book Burkett shows you specifically what to do about your situation. The stories he shares of others who have worked through their struggles is an encouragement.

Food

Food is probably the single area where we save the most money (other than diapers—more on that later). When I worked full-time, it was normal for us to eat at a restaurant two or three times per week. Our monthly food outlay for the two of us was $200 per month higher than what I now spend for the seven of us. After coming home to be a full-time mom, we saved money on food since I did all our cooking. Over a period of years I developed my culinary skills to cook from scratch, buy food in bulk, and make my own bread. Our garden also adds to our food dollar savings.

I find that particularly in the area of food, a little planning is worth a lot of money. If the children and I are going out and there is any chance we will not make it home for a meal, I bring something with us. To simplify the matter, it is most often a loaf of bread, peanut butter and jelly, raw carrots, and a big jug of water with cups. If I fail to do this and we stop for fast food, it costs us a minimum of $15.00 and we are usually still hungry.

I am also saving money by making my own baby food. With my oldest child I remember vividly how our shopping cart was filled with dozens of little baby food jars. Now I know that these are totally unnecessary. I buy a large can of peaches, pears, or plums to puree in the blender. What is not eaten is frozen in an ice cube tray for later use. We also mash up whatever we are eating and feed it to the baby.

Shopping with a list helps reduce the amount of money you spend on food. I have a clipboard with a calculator attached so I can add up the total as I shop. Be flexible regarding sale items and coupons that will help fill your food storage, but keep focused on your list. Just recently I shopped without a list. I did not buy anything frivolous or expensive. I estimated the cost of the items in my head. When the total was rung up I was surprised at the bill. It was three times what I usually spend. By not using a list, I lost track of my expenditures.

Use coupons when possible. I don't use them a lot because I find buying in bulk through food co-ops and wholesale clubs to be more cost effective. Many coupons are for prepared foods we don't use. Sometimes I will find a good coupon that, paired up with an in-store sale, makes a great buy. Buy the smallest size of the product when using coupons. A 50¢ off coupon on a 100 oz. bottle of Tide at $5 will yield a 10 percent savings. Using the same coupon on the 200 oz. bottle at $10 would only yield a 5 percent savings. You need to calculate the per-ounce cost of the small and the large size after the coupon to see which is better. The largest package is *not* always the best buy anyway. Mike Yorkey's book *Saving Money Any Way You Can* talks extensively about coupon use.

Buying items in bulk really helps the budget. Even for a small family, this is a good approach. I buy one small package of an item such as shampoo or dish soap. I keep these small containers handy and refill them from an economy-size container when they run out. You can also buy a large package containing many bars of soap and just store them until you use them since they do not spoil. This saves time as well as money since you will buy soap infrequently.

Take advantage of opportunities to buy fresh produce in bulk. Farmer's markets are a great place to negotiate a wholesale price on a large purchase. Last summer I was able to buy ten dozen ears of sweet corn at $1.50 per dozen. The going price that day was over $2 a dozen. It was fairly simple to blanch and freeze the corn. Frozen corn in the store was expensive one winter due to crop failures. Even if you can't use such a large quantity, surely you can find a few people who could split it with you. It also helps to get to know the produce manager of your favorite store. Often he will let you know when reduced produce will be available or will possibly offer to sell you at reduced cost produce that the store is throwing away. Larger chain stores sometimes have policies against this, but the ma and pa grocery stores still consider these options.

You should set aside some area of your living space to store such items. We have a dry crawl space that we use for storage. It is cool in the winter and affords us a "root cellar" to keep produce in over the cold months. Currently we have oranges, grapefruit, sweet potatoes, and pecans that are doing well. A portion of a laundry room, attached garage, or spare closet are other possibilities. I find great freedom in having a well-stocked home. We seldom run out of the items kept in storage because we replenish when items are running low. This need not take up a lot of space and can be on a small scale or as grand a storage plan as you can manage.

Diapers

Just this week I realized that by shopping good sales and using some $2 off coupons, I have stocked up on enough diapers to last us through the next year. (We only use disposables occasionally, so it is not as many bags as you might think.) I stored diapers for our baby several months before she was born. Since we have a budgeted monthly allotment for diapers and toilet paper, I told my husband we could eliminate that allotment. This was exciting for me because this was the first time I had been able to reduce my portion of the budget. We are so trimmed down on expenses that it is getting tough to cut more. By storing diapers that I purchased very inexpensively (two for one sale), I eliminated the time it takes to watch sales as well as the money we were setting aside for them.

Our need for disposable diapers is greatly reduced by our use of cloth diapers. I have had one or more children in diapers for ten years. If I had used disposables all of that time, I would have spent between $4,000 and $4,500 on them. The longer I use cloth diapers, the more convinced I am that disposables are only good for special circumstances (for example, church). Most of the time I prefer to use cloth. I understand that babies in a day-care setting may be required to have disposables, but if your little ones are with you, they can wear cloth. When my oldest child was born, I heard a media report that cloth diapers and disposables cost about the same when you factor in the cost of purchasing the cloth diapers and laundering them. Being a new mom, I just accepted this and was not motivated to use cloth all of the time. Finally, Jim tallied the cost of washing one load of diapers. He calculated the cost of the hot water, electricity, and laundry soap (the most expensive component). We found that it only cost $1 to wash a load of diapers! I only wash diapers once a week (even for more than one in diapers). I do not soak them or double rinse them. They turn out fine. Not one of my children has had a problem with rashes from cloth diapers.

It is worth the investment to buy diaper service quality diapers. I use these as the outside diaper and then a less expensive diaper for a liner (I always double diaper). Diaper services will sometimes sell used diapers or you can purchase them new from Equipping the Family (P.O. Box 3202, Glen Ellyn, IL 60138-3202; phone: 630-588-0211). The diapers I prefer are now being used for the third child. They hold up well. Regular-sized diapers are available as well as a smaller size that is great for newborns.

Cloth diapers are a huge money-saver. It gets even better when you find six dozen new cloth diapers at a garage sale and get them for $1.50 a dozen. (I have only had this happen once in *many* years of garage sales.) These are great liners inside the diaper service diapers. I don't use a diaper service because it is very expensive to pay them to wash the diapers. But if you have more money than time, you should check into a diaper service as an alternative to disposable diapers.

There are other savings in relationship to diapering the baby. I no longer use diaper wipes unless we are out of the home. I had a lot of old washcloths I was not using. I now wet them and store them in an old diaper wipe plastic container and leave it on the changing table. These are much more efficient at cleaning up the big messes and are not so irritating to a baby's bottom. I simply toss them in the diaper pail and wash them with the cloth diapers. I still take wipes with me when we go out, but I go through them very slowly.

Toiletries are also an area that can be trimmed down. Baby powder is not necessary and can be harmful to babies. Powders containing talc should be avoided because of their adverse effect on the lungs. Cornstarch is preferred if you want to use powder. Diaper rash creams are expensive and contain only one ingredient that is really necessary. I prefer to buy a tube of zinc oxide at a much lower cost. The results are the same.

Utilities

We have experimented with reducing our utility bills through a variety of means. We strive to use our utilities as little as possible. We have trained our children not to use lights when the sun is shining. We turn lights off when nobody is in the room. It is cheaper to turn lights on and off than it is to leave them on for hours. We enjoy the use of our oil lamps at the dinner table, which eliminates lights in our whole house for about an hour each evening. In the summer, when it gets very hot, we will turn our air conditioning on for one day and then turn it off the next day while leaving the windows closed. This works pretty well.

Before the arrival of our wood-burning stove, we turned our heat on as late in the season as possible and turned it off as early in the spring as we could. Lest you think that these reductions in creature comfort have been easy for me, let me update you on the wood-burning stove. I really do like the stove. When the temperature is above 20 degrees F outside it heats the whole house like a champ! My zealous husband finds it comfortable no matter what the outside temperature. This has led to some heated discussions on how much heat we need. This morning it was 15 below zero when I woke up (that was outside—not in my house!). We have had to compromise and use our heat during this cold snap. I am committed to cutting back our expenses, but sometimes the level of discomfort my husband is willing to experience far exceeds my own (as usual, the children are thriving—I'm the one who doesn't want to change). I share this with you because you may not be willing to do some of the things I am suggesting because they are just too uncomfortable for you. A friend who is the mother of seven only uses disposable diapers. That's okay. We are all different. You must decide what ideas you are comfortable with and do them. Something that you cannot fathom right now may be just what you need in five years. I again encourage you to view our family story as a springboard for your own ideas. You are smart and creative and probably can improve upon some of my suggestions.

Appliances

Appliances are not made as well as they used to be. Plastic parts have replaced metal parts in many machines. I do not believe this to be a good thing. It is almost as if appliances are being made to last only a short time, so that you have to replace them. Jim was repairing a microwave for someone and found out when purchasing the parts that the new microwaves have a much shorter life expectancy than the older models. Ours was twelve years old, and we never had a problem with it. Our friend's is only a few years old.

One way to get around this problem is to buy used appliances. If you have access to someone who is handy at fixing things, this is the way to go. If not, consider training yourself through a class or a do-it-yourself book. Our local recycling center has "book rescue" days where you can pick up books free of charge. I picked up a five-volume *Homeowner's Encyclopedia* from one of them. People throw away appliances that need minor repairs because it is cheaper to buy a new one than to pay a repair bill. It is cheaper still to just fix it yourself and only have to buy the parts. Our gas grill came from the garbage needing a knob that cost under $2.

When purchasing used appliances, be sure to ask questions. Don't just ask how old the washing machine is but how many people are in the family. The wear and tear on a machine with one or two people in the family is much different than the wear and tear on my washing machine. If you are buying a stove, ask if the people cook often or if they eat out frequently. A five-year-old stove may be virtually brand-new if they seldom used it.

Excess Goods and Services

Another way to save money is to reevaluate the goods and services that you use. Do you really need call waiting? Is cable TV necessary? Even though these are not expensive services, they add up. A good way to evaluate how much you need something is to get rid of it. It may cost you to reinstate a service such as call waiting, but you won't know what you can live without until you get rid of it. I sense that many of us are so used to modern conveniences that we don't realize how many things we don't really need. Ask yourself questions. Do I really need an electric can opener, or can I open cans by hand? Is the garage door opener essential, or could I use the exercise of getting out of the car and opening the door? There are no right or wrong answers here. It all depends on what your family finds suitable. We own a snow-blower. Given all that you know about us, you may think that is silly. We have reasons for owning one, but these reasons may not apply to you. (Actually, my husband may be thinking about selling this next—who knows?)

Before I let you in on my favorite money-saving activity, here are a few odds and ends that we have realized are helpful in reducing our expenditures. Date nights with our spouse can be fairly expensive after factoring in the cost of the baby-sitting. About a year ago we discovered the joy of "going out" by staying in. Our daughters were six and eight years old at the time. We ordered Chinese food after the little ones were in bed, and our daughters dressed up to be our waitresses. They set the table, presented the food, and cleaned up the mess! We enjoyed it very much. And they were pleased with the tip we gave them.

Be creative! Most of the time you can do what you want to do at a fraction of the cost if you just think about it long enough.

Birthday parties are a good example. If you choose to have a party at a fast-food establishment, it can easily cost you $75 or more before you are done. We recently had a lovely birthday party with ten girls in attendance. We made very nice hats for each of them to take home for their American Girl dolls. The girls had fun and went home with a useful gift, and we only spent $25 on everything. I'm sure it could be done for even less than that.

Garage Sales

My favorite way to save money is to take in garage sales. The tremendous bargains I have found are too numerous to list. I have found that with a little forethought, I don't really need to shop much in stores anymore. It helps to know a little about how to garage sale effectively.

I make a list of whatever we want—regardless of the cost. This way I know what everyone in the family needs or wants. It is no longer unusual for me to find something at a garage sale that we could only afford if it was purchased this way. I keep a running list of our needs/wants just like I would keep a shopping list. I include sizes, colors, and other pertinent information. This winter I am wearing a coat that is exactly what I had described on my list. It cost me a fraction of the original retail price. I also have a juicer that is just what I wanted. It took two years before I found one, but because I had listed the make and model on my list, I knew a good deal when I found it. I paid 25 percent of the retail value for a perfectly good machine.

Share your list with a friend. We have so many sales in our area, it is impossible to go to them all. Many times people sell things inexpensively just to get rid of them. If other people know of your needs, they can help. I look for big-ticket items for people and have asked to borrow a phone at a garage sale to check with my friend before I buy. I will be looking for bunk beds this summer, and I am confident that this method will help me find them. If you are at a good sale (especially clothing), leave your name and number for leftovers after the sale. In our area, clothing does not sell well anymore because there are so many people selling clothes. This is an excellent way to outfit your family. I have many new maternity clothes that I found at garage sales. Most of them were better than what I already owned. Garage sales are a good way to upgrade your clothing and your baby equipment. Boldly offer less than the marked price. This is expected at garage sales. Sometimes you can get some things free if you are buying a lot of things from one sale. We bought two Singer Touch and Sew sewing machines at the garage sale where we purchased our chain saw. We only paid $10 apiece for the machines.

Neighborhood garage sales are excellent. Go on the first day of the sale; get there a little early. Rainy and cold days offer good bargains since less people go out on those days. I enjoy going to garage sales. I have saved our family so much money that I cannot afford to stay home. It actually takes less time to garage sale than to shop in stores. I am often disappointed by the quality and selection that I find in stores. I do better at garage sales where I often find salesman's samples that are brand-new.

Sewing

I make clothes that are not labor-intensive. Many jumper patterns are very simple and can be made fairly quickly. My daughters and I enjoy wearing matching clothes. Recently all seven of us were matching in a family picture. We all wore the same color T-shirt with the girls wearing matching vests. The baby wore a jumper made out of the same material as the vest. This did not take a long time but had a very desirable outcome.

Sewing is not difficult with a few basic instructions. Fabric stores offer sewing classes for adults and children. Used sewing machines can be purchased inexpensively. With an investment of just a little time and money, you can begin to sew nice clothing. A beginning project of a simple jumper without buttons or a zipper can be a great encouragement for you.

Freebies

The next best thing to garage sales is getting something free. When you let family and friends know what you are looking for, it is likely that someone will meet that need. We have received canning supplies on more than one occasion because someone knew we canned. Don't be ashamed to ask for things! Remember that our free wood is worth almost $2,000. We had a $500 vacuum given to us that needed some minor repairs.

Free instruction is helpful too. Ask people you meet how to do things. I asked a lady who sold lovely bouquets at our farmer's market how to grow flowers. We had planted seeds for a cutting garden but had no results. I learned that it is best to start flowers from seed in the house and then transplant them. It was just a casual conversation, but it yielded some useful information.

Do It Yourself

The more you can learn to do for yourself, the more money you will save. Even if you are not a handy person, you can learn to do more for yourself. It is helpful before hiring outside help to ask yourself the question "Can *I* do this?" If the answer is yes, you must follow up with "Do I have time to do it?" Saving money most often is a balance between time and money. For our family, we have decided to do as much as we can ourselves so we don't require as much money. We cut all of our own hair. The boys have simple crew cuts, and the girls all have long hair that just needs to be trimmed. Jim does the maintenance and car repairs. He also does our home improvements. His latest job has been to cut and split all of the wood for our wood-burning stove. If tough economic times are ahead, this may be a sound approach for everyone.

As I have said before, you really have to decide what makes the most sense for your family. You need to assess where you are and where you want to be. I believe that many, if not most, working mothers in two-income households could come home fulltime if they wanted to. That probably would require a drastic lifestyle adjustment, but it could be done. Once you begin to eliminate the costs of paying others (day care, restaurant, cleaners, etc.) to do what you can do yourself, leaving your job becomes a real possibility.

By implementing strategies I have outlined here, you can reduce your family's living expenses. All of us can benefit from being more prudent in our financial matters. Even the smallest changes can impact your family. As you actively become more conservative in your spending, you may be surprised at just how much you don't need to get by.

6

Holidays and Gift Giving

THE CELEBRATION OF HOLIDAYS AND THE GIFT GIVING THAT WE experience throughout the year are times to consider saving time and money. Our tendency is to try to take in all of the great activities and buy all of the wonderful bargains we can to celebrate these times. I know—I have done this myself. One Christmas I particularly had difficulty with time management. The following story explains it all.

It was after a hectic weekend two weeks before Christmas that I realized something was wrong. We were so busy that I had a difficult time enjoying our activities because I was organizing details in my mind—what to have for dinner, what clothing all of us needed for our next activity, etc. After three days and nights of back-to-back events, I prayed that the next day I would be a Mary instead of a Martha.

It was amazing how the details of the next day played themselves out. It began in the morning when one of our rabbits jumped out of her cage, and my daughter could not get her back in. Jamie (who was eight years old at the time) yelled for help for twenty minutes before Jim finally figured out she had been outside too long. Next we left for church a little early in order to first attend a "Christmas on the Farm" day at a local 1890s working farm. When it came time for us to leave (already late for church), our van became stuck in the parking lot. I got out to push, and mud splattered all over my wool coat. We arrived at church half an hour late.

Later in the afternoon we had company coming over for a cookie exchange. Jim finally found the Christmas decorations fifteen minutes after the guests were scheduled to arrive. They helped us put some of them up. Later in the evening my oldest daughter was baptized at our church. We had dinner at 9:00 that evening at a local restaurant.

This is not at all a typical day for our family. We make every effort to keep our days to a manageable level of activity. Why, then, do we set ourselves up like the scenario above during the holiday season? How can we ever be a Mary when we have so many details to work out?

The story of Mary and Martha is one of my favorites in the whole Bible. In Luke 10:38-42 we read of two sisters who approached life very differently. Mary sat at Jesus' feet listening to Him speak, while Martha was distracted by all the preparations that needed to be made. Jesus made a comment to Martha that fits so well for many of us during the holiday season. "Martha, Martha," the Lord answered, "you are worried and upset about many things, but only one thing is needed. Mary has chosen what is better, and it will not be taken away from her."

These are powerful words that need to be applied to each of the days of our lives. But how do we ever make this work during the holidays? There are so many things that we have to do! We must make or buy presents, bake cookies, decorate both the inside and outside of our house, participate in the children's Christmas program, visit all our relatives—and the list goes on! Do we really need to do all these things? Would eliminating half of them be enough? If we truly do desire to be more like Mary and listen to the words of our Lord, what should we do about all of the details that are a part of a busy mom's holiday season?

I want to encourage you first by saying, you will not be able to make all of the needed changes the first year. We had been adapting our holiday season for a few years and finally felt pretty good about our plans between Thanksgiving and New Year's Day. That was until I had two different kinds of flu during the month of December. (I had been ill three times in three months—ever since I wrote the chapter on building your immune system!) My illnesses further simplified our plans, and we were delighted with the results. Here are some of the changes we have made to simplify this busy time and put the joy back into our days.

First, we have established limits in many areas. We have eliminated just about all the traditional holiday decorations. (Don't panic! This is just what we have done. By all means keep yours if they are a joy for your family.) After studying the origins of traditions such as Christmas trees and the use of evergreens in decorating, we determined that for our family we would be better off with a few candles. As difficult as it seemed at first, getting rid of all my handmade Christmas crafts has been a great blessing. I am not storing all of this stuff that only comes out for six weeks each year. I am not setting up and taking down all of these things either. I am now free to do some simple holiday decorating each year. This year we enjoyed the few candles that were set out. Since I was sick, that is all we were able to do. Next year we will do more, creatively tailoring our decorations to be appropriate to leave up all winter. I do enjoy seeing my infant and toddler roaming freely in my living room without fear of reprimand for getting mixed up in the lights, the tinsel, or the tree.

We are also limiting our gift giving. For three years we have made most of our gifts, which has helped with the budget. This past year we decided not to exchange gifts within our immediate family (there are seven of us!). Our rationale was basically twofold. Primarily, we felt that since we meet the needs of our children throughout the year, it did not make sense to hold back things like socks and underwear so they could receive them in their stocking. In addition, it was becoming increasingly more difficult to keep the gifts for five children balanced in terms of value per child and also the number of gifts being the same. That had made me downright irritated the previous year, and I realized this was ridiculous.

Before you think we are cruel parents, here is what we did instead. Wonderful presents were received from both sets of grandparents so the children did have much to open. We offered them the gift of our time. The children were very excited because instead of receiving gifts from Mom and Dad, they received Mom and Dad! Each child chose an activity to be done with either Mom or Dad. My oldest daughter, Jamie, chose a train ride into the city of Chicago to spend the day with Dad. Jenny chose to go out to lunch with Mom and then shopping (somehow this seems like a great gift for me too!). My boys, Jimmy and Jonathan (aged three and four), chose to go to McDonald's Playland (a *big* deal since we don't frequent McDonald's). A good time was had by all!

Secondly, we are committed to keeping our focus on relationships. Christmas is a celebration of the birth of the most important man (who is also fully God) who ever lived. There is no better way to celebrate than to do what Jesus says in His Word! In Matthew 22:37-40 we read, "Jesus replied: 'Love the Lord your God with all your heart and with all your soul and with all your mind.' This is the first and greatest commandment. And the second is like it: 'Love your neighbor as yourself.' All the Law and the Prophets hang on these two commandments." Our family helps deliver Christmas baskets to less fortunate families in our area. The Salvation Army coordinates a large effort, and nearly 150 families receive food, clothing, and presents each year. Our children participate in helping carry the gifts into the homes of the people who receive them. Even our two-year-old helped by carrying a roll of paper towels or a package of toilet paper. Our children did this with love in their heart, wanting to help each family we met. The smiles on the faces of the children receiving the gifts was witnessed by my own children. This is what I want my children to know about Christmas.

Relationships with friends and family should come first during the holiday season. They are important year-round, of course, but at holiday time these relationships need to take precedence over any holiday preparations. Relationships don't just flourish because it is Christmas. Many, if not most, families have relational issues that need to be worked through before gathering as a group for the holidays. Failure to do so creates tension and most certainly takes our focus away from Christ and the meaning His life and death have for us. We read in Matthew 5:23-24 these words of Jesus: "Therefore, if you are offering your gift at the altar and there remember that your brother has something against you, leave your gift there in front of the altar. First go and be reconciled to your brother; then come and offer your gift." Not being reconciled with our brother (friends, family, neighbors, etc.) makes loving our neighbor as ourselves impossible. Another verse that addresses such situations is found in Hebrews 12:14: "Make every effort to live in peace with all men." Another is: "If it is possible, as far as it depends on you, live at peace with everyone" (Romans 12:18). We do not control the responses of others, but we can choose to do what is right ourselves in the eyes of the Lord.

Another challenge we have experienced with relationships involves the issue of time. Have you ever noticed that many people are so busy shopping and going to activities that there is little time to socialize? We have people in for a cookie exchange each year and try also to have a Christmas caroling party if the weather permits. By setting up our home as a warm place to stop for a visit, we hope to offer a peaceful alternative to the frantic days before Christmas.

A discussion of holidays would not be complete without

reviewing just how our Christmas celebration really went this year. Pay close attention to my plans versus how things actually turned out.

We send out an annual letter each year at Christmas. Ideally we enclose a family picture. I decided that this letter should go out at Thanksgiving to better utilize my time in December. This year, for the first time since its inception, there was no annual letter. I just never got to it. Plans for next year include a different time for the annual letter to go out. That is one problem solved!

Christmas dinner was interesting this year too. We eat dinner at my parents' house and always have a feast. This year we had some challenges. The master turkey chef (my dad) had the flu. My mom made a great turkey herself, but the foil pan had a hole in it, and much grease had dripped out before my mom noticed it. Before the fire department was needed, Dad came to the rescue. The noodles that my mom makes from scratch turned into one big glop in the pot of water because it wasn't boiling when she dropped them in. She had to start over. Christmas morning I called to say that some of what I had said I was bringing never got made. I *always* have homemade cookies to share. This year we had very few cookies. My mom said that was fine, just bring the pumpkin pies. She also asked me if it was okay to make corn casserole. I said fine.

I went off to make the pumpkin pies, and she went off to make the corn casserole. Then I discovered that I had no pumpkin and she discovered that her frozen corn did not seem right, so she tossed it into the garbage. She made some cauliflower instead, and my girls made one apple pie (we only had one egg). I know I sound pretty disorganized, and I was this year. I had been sick, and we had gone out to some activities, and I just did not have a handle on things. Our dinner at my mom's was great, but it got me thinking about potlucks, especially for large families. It seems to me that it would be fun to treat holiday dinners as potlucks so the burden of all of the meal doesn't rest with one or two people. That would help us keep focused more on people than on food. (More Mary, less Martha.)

Keeping focused on people in the area of gift giving is an art. So often it seems that we make or buy what we think they should have instead of what would make them happy. By thinking of the person and their interests, we are better able to give them suitable gifts. I find that gift giving is much more fun if it is considered throughout the calendar year and not just at Christmas. Gift giving is so important that I would like to examine it in detail.

It helps to know why we are giving gifts. If we are simply meeting an obligation (such as exchanging gifts at Christmas), the process becomes a chore. In November I enjoyed the discussion my table of ladies at MOPs (Mothers of Preschoolers) had regarding Christmas gift giving. It seemed that this area of holiday preparation was difficult for most everyone at the table. The expectations of others, budgets, time to make gifts, and quantity of gifts to get were all discussed. It seemed that we all were less than satisfied with the way gift giving was being handled. It made me realize that *why* we give gifts is as important as the gift.

The greatest gift of all comes to mind as a model for modern-day gift giving: "For God so loved the world that he gave his one and only Son, that whoever believes in him shall not perish but have eternal life" (John 3:16). Jesus is a gift for all who receive Him. We have been offered this gift from a God who loves us so much that He willingly sacrificed His *only* Son so He could take the punishment for our wrongs. God's gift of Jesus was a result of His love for us and involved a sacrifice on His part for our benefit. I believe that the only *true* gifts we give are those that come from our heart. Anything less is merely the giving of stuff from one person to another.

Over time I have found that making the presents I give are the best way for me to give from my heart. It is too easy to race to the store and grab the first thing you see. It takes sacrifice to think of the gift, buy the materials, make the gift yourself, and give it.

Since gift giving takes place all year long, we will now take our focus off of the holidays (December is only a twelfth of the year) and put it on how to manage the giving of gifts all year long.

There are many reasons to give a gift. A gift can show appreciation for what the hostess has done in preparing for her guests. Appreciation gifts can affirm a teacher's efforts in educating your child. Birthday gifts are special acknowledgments of the wonderful day in history when the recipient of the gift was born. Anniversary gifts are a good way to honor our parents (and, of course, our spouses). Some holidays lend themselves to gift giving— for example, Valentine's Day. (I think this is my mother-in-law's favorite holiday.) Whatever the reason, giving a gift is a special exchange that can warm the hearts of both giver and receiver.

I love to work on crafts, but with time in short supply, it seems the only time I do crafts is when making a gift for someone. I truly enjoy the work that goes into the making of the gift, and I know when the gift is given that I have made it just for that person. Since I like gifts to serve a function, I consider the needs of the receiver. An elderly person confined to bed or a chair would enjoy something pretty to look at—perhaps a picture drawn or painted by your child. A new mother (or an older mother like me with a lot of children) appreciates labor-saving gifts such as a meal, housecleaning, or a gift mix. Children love to receive art supplies they can use for creative play.

About now you must be wondering how I could find time to make all of these gifts. The truth is, I don't. I *make* the time. I also organize myself in ways that spread out the gift-making process throughout the entire year. I am still developing in this area. I hope in the future to have gifts made for people a few months before their special day. In the meantime I have some techniques that make gift making fairly simple with little time, money, or talent available. I mention talent because I don't believe you have to be very gifted to make gifts. Some crafts are so simple that my children show me how to do them.

I make a point of finding gift ideas that are quick and easy. By far my best source of inspiration has been the craft time at my MOPs (Mother of Preschoolers) meetings. We only have about half an hour to finish our crafts, so each one is quick. The projects are also very affordable. Sometimes there are extra craft kits that I will purchase at a nominal cost and put in a box for future use (making sure I label the box). Often my girls will put together the extra kits that I purchase. Each week our craft has an instruction sheet that I file in a plastic sleeve and put in a three-ring binder marked "Crafts." This not only provides me with a handy reference of tried and true gift ideas but also limits the clutter of magazines that may only contain one or two craft ideas that I need. I have cut out instructions from magazines and newspapers and have brought home free flyers from craft stores. I store all of these instructions in my binder. My children have also begun to cut out pictures from specialty magazines (the ones that are adorable but mostly unaffordable for many of us) and glue them on a piece of white paper to put in the craft notebook. Many of these high-priced items are very easy to make when you can copy the picture. This may seem like a lot of work, but in reality I only spend a minute or two here and there working on these things.

What takes more time is keeping my craft supplies in order. I think I have finally gotten this under control. In our last house I had to store my supplies in different locations in the house. This did not work well because I never knew what I had. I now have all my supplies under my bed in cardboard boxes. The side of each box has a label to indicate what is in each box. Through garage sales and a few stores going out of business I have accumulated quite a bit. But it does me no good if I cannot find it. It helps to have a list in your purse of what items you could use more of and those that you are overstocked on. This helps keep spending in line when super-sales happen.

Purchasing craft supplies at garage sales or store-closing sales can greatly reduce the cost of the gifts you make. Although the gifts you make should be nice ones, they don't have to be expensive. Last summer I found a lot of silk flowers for about 10¢ apiece. Many stems were originally $2 or more in the store. I only bought the colors I liked and now have a great selection. A couple of years ago a local fabric store decided to get rid of some of their inventory that had been around for two or three years to make room for new fabric. I was able to buy some baby quilt panels for $3. They usually cost $10 to $12. It doesn't take much time at all to sew some bias tape around the edge and so make a special gift. I also got a lifetime supply of no-sew transfers at 75 percent off when a local store closed. Ironing a transfer onto a T-shirt or sweatshirt and then painting it goes quickly. I enjoy doing this, and the gifts turn out great.

Sometimes it is not so easy to decide what to make for someone. There are many ways to get good ideas. Ask people questions about items they have that you find interesting. A friend from MOPs had solved a window treatment dilemma in exactly the way I wanted to solve mine. I asked her specific details about how the window treatment was made. Even though this was not for a gift, the principle still applies. Observe people who have a natural talent at developing gift ideas. Read crafting magazines. *Crafting Traditions* by Reiman Publications is an excellent resource. It could be beneficial to share a subscription with a friend. It wouldn't hurt to invest in a few good gift idea books also. This past year I purchased *The Perfect Mix, 90 Gift-Giving Ideas for Bread, Soup, Dessert, and Other Homemade Mixes* by Diane Phillips. I made up some bean soup mixes and put them in decorated brown bags. I stored them in a basket near the front door, and any visitors during the month of December received a little gift. This book is versatile, and I will be using it for many years. I also found an expensive gift idea book at a garage sale for $1. The instructions are simple and fully illustrated.

Craft shows are another source of inspiration for me. Some of the items I see there are simple to make. Sometimes I will buy one to serve as a model if I don't think I will remember how to make it. I carry a small notebook with me to jot down ideas. As long as you don't stand right in front of the vendor taking notes, they usually don't mind. You aren't copying their ideas to make and sell them. You just want to make a few gifts.

Another page in your small notebook could be for a list of the people you buy for on a regular basis. Write down ideas for their gifts as soon as you think of them so you aren't trying to remember later when gift giving time rolls around.

It helps to take advantage of special purchases. We spent Thanksgiving in Dallas, Texas, last year and came home with a case of oranges, a case of grapefruit, and fourteen pounds of thin shelled pecans. These were all in season and were purchased at a great price. When we arrived home, I got to thinking that we would not be able to eat all of the fruit. I decided to make fruit baskets for four of our neighbors. I had fun making them, and they looked pretty good. I never could have afforded to buy such a gift, but because I had the fruit, I was able to put them together. Whenever I see potential gift materials at garage sales, I think through my plans for that year and purchase what I can use. Sometimes a deal is too good to refuse, and I end up planning the gift around the materials I have found.

I know this sounds ultra-organized, but it really isn't hard. It is just like stocking your pantry with food. Instead, you are preparing your craft supply box to meet your needs the next time you make a gift. Your craft notebook supplies the ideas, sales provide materials, and you take an hour or two out of your busy life and enjoy making something for someone else. I think the favorite gift that I make takes only a few minutes. I have pre-washed Onezies in size medium. I iron on a design that is suitable for a boy or a girl. I paint the outside of the design and paint a heart on the back. That's it. It costs about $2 apiece, and I can afford to give more baby gifts this way. It is a personal gift, and the feedback I have received has been positive.

One thank you card stands out in my mind. I made one of these shirts for a fellow firefighter on my husband's shift. He and his wife were proud parents of their first child, a baby girl. Previously this man had little interest in talk about children or family life. All of that changed with the birth of his daughter. The thank you card we received was written by the man. On one side of the card he wrote a note to my children that was from his daughter. At the bottom, he enclosed a clipping of her hair. The note for us was very nice also.

Since I have $300 per year as my entire gift giving budget, I have learned to be frugal in the making of these gifts. Some gifts are still bought at the store, but most are homemade. I learned after the first year of trying to make all Christmas gifts right before Christmas that it just doesn't work for me. The only way to keep up is to make them all year round. I find it motivating to make gifts at the time I am inspired—after returning from a craft show, for example. If I have just gotten a good deal on supplies, that is a great time to assemble them. As a home schooler I find there are some days that don't work well with the lesson plans I have made. Regardless of the reason, it works well for our whole family to just shift gears and make some gifts that day.

This same theory holds true when kids are home in the summer and need some structure to keep their day going. You can set up an assembly line and make a number of the same gift to store in a box ready for gift giving. It streamlines everything if you keep supplies ready to use—laminated gift tags, decorated paper bags, fabric that is already ironed onto Heat n Bond or Wonder Under for use on the Onezies. I try to aim for the simple gifts—the ones you are likely to finish. In addition to keeping our gift giving box stocked with gifts that are finished, I desire to have Christmas gifts all done before Thanksgiving. I haven't managed this yet, but I am still trying.

Gift giving doesn't have to be expensive. It can be an enjoyable opportunity to create something to give from your heart.

There are many ways to attempt to do this. I have mentioned only a few. Examine your own interests and talents, and see what you can offer as a gift. Do you love to cook? Give a meal. Do you like to care for children? Give the gift of child-care. Do you know how to prepare income taxes? Give the gift of your time to do someone's taxes. There are endless possibilities. As you forget about shopping at the store and think about other alternatives, it is amazing how many there actually are.

My oldest daughter showed me just how special creative gift giving can be. Even though we did not formally exchange gifts last Christmas, she gave each one of us a coupon. She thought about the responsibilities of the receiver and offered to do a job for them for a specified time. All of the gift coupons were specifically designed to lighten the receiver's load. My coupon was for "planning the meals for a week." This was truly a gift from the heart.

7

Chores, Cleaning, and Laundry

IN OUR FAMILY WE HAVE A WORK ETHIC. EVERYONE DOWN TO the one-year-old plays a role in helping with each day's work. It has to be that way in order for our home to run smoothly. Moreover, I think it *should be* that way for optimal results in the training of our children.

Genesis 3:19 says, "By the sweat of your brow you will eat your food until you return to the ground, since from it you were taken; for dust you are and to dust you will return." One of the consequences of the sin committed by Adam and Eve in the Garden of Eden is that we must work. Whether for pay or not, we all must work. It is good for our children to learn this truth at an early age when their attitude toward work is being shaped. Have you ever been around adults who complain endlessly about having to work? Chances are, these people were not required to work as children. When young ones have everything done for them and are not required to work in any way, they fail to learn the rewards of hard labor. As adults they continue to expect others to do for them what they could do for themselves. Proverbs 10:4 says, "Lazy hands make a man poor, but diligent hands bring wealth."

I don't believe children are born with a tendency toward laziness. On the contrary, I have found that very young children are most eager to help whenever they can. Proverbs 13:4 has helped me keep my focus: "The sluggard craves and gets nothing, but the desires of the diligent are fully satisfied." At two years old my Jonathan was very interested in vacuuming. He was not very skilled at first, but I let him do it. As he nears his fourth birthday, he is as eager as ever to help. It is important for us to nurture this desire to help as soon as it manifests itself. In this way we are helping develop the character quality of diligence in our sons and daughters early on. Although very young children cannot do much by themselves, they can do much as an assistant to an older child or a parent. The entire family benefits from such an approach. Parents no longer work endless hours while children play from dawn until dusk. The family that works together has time to play together and in so doing builds deep relationships with each other.

If you don't instill a love for work in your children while they are young, it will be more difficult to do so later on. My oldest two children at ages seven and nine have reached a point at which many children balk at helping around the home. I believe that we too would be experiencing the same attitudes had we not implemented the strategies I will outline for you. This is not to say that we will never come up against a complaining spirit, but I can say that so far our children are all eager to work. The biggest issue we have is when someone becomes dissatisfied with his own particular work assignment. This is corrected easily by reassigning tasks periodically.

I am especially grateful to the Fahey family in New York. As I have mentioned, we were able to spend one week on their homestead and observe the day-to-day operation of their family. Their workload was substantial, but each family member had his or her role to play in the work for each day. Teamwork was essential and worked quite well. We came home determined to implement this in our own young family. The results have surpassed my greatest hopes. Be encouraged as I share some practical ways to handle the work that needs to be done each day in your home.

Typically children talk about (or should I say, complain about) chores as something to get done quickly so they can do something else. In looking at the definition of the word *chore* I found that it can mean "an unpleasant task."[1] Certainly all of us can relate to unpleasant tasks that are a part of our work routine. They are not all unpleasant though. I believe that the word *chore* is a poor one to use when describing the work we must do. *Chore* has a negative connotation and does not encourage cheerful, willing compliance. If my husband wanted me to add some bit of work to my schedule and announced, "Honey, I have a new chore for you!" I'm sure my response would not be enthusiastic. I'm not sure I would do my best work on something that was introduced as a chore.

The same holds true with our children. If we want them to work cheerfully and willingly, we need to introduce their work in a positive way. Just recently we have replaced the term *chore* with the word *service*. Each child has certain tasks that are to be performed as that child's service. Now, just who is that child serving? It could be a number of different people. Most importantly it is the Lord Jesus Christ. In Colossians 3:23-24 we read, "Whatever you do, work at it with all your heart, as working for the Lord, not for men,, since you know that you will receive an inheritance from the Lord as a reward. It is the Lord Christ you are serving."

I refer to this verse often. We moms are expected to perform many mundane tasks. I don't need to list them. You know them by heart. It is easy to complain about these tasks if our attitudes are not right. By remembering that even in the routine work we do, we are serving Christ, we can humble ourselves and do our work joyfully. I will admit that diaper changing is not the most exciting part of my service list. I do know that I have been doing it for the last ten years straight, and if I let myself see diapering as negative, it would hamper me in completing this task that is done many times each day. This will be true for your children too. If they see their work negatively, they will have a more difficult time accomplishing it.

You may be wondering how a child can be cheerful while doing a distasteful task. The best way I can explain this is to share what my own children are doing. By God's grace this is one area of family life that we seem to have begun properly. The story begins with the diligence of my husband when our oldest, Jamie, was about two years old. One two-year-old can make quite a mess and without the help of siblings has a big task ahead at cleanup time. It is not unusual for a parent to pick up toys for such a wee one. Jim had a better idea and worked with Jamie to pick up her toys. I had a newborn, and at the end of the day I felt no inclination to work with Jamie picking up toys. It is good for the husband or someone other than yourself (possibly an older sibling) to work on this project.

Patiently, Jim helped direct her in putting her toys away. It takes more time to train the oldest child, but they in turn help train younger siblings to help clean up. I do not clean up toys at our house. The children play with them, and they are expected to put them away. It helps that we do not allow them to pull out everything at once. If only a few toys are out, it is much easier to clean up. Not long ago we allowed our three- and five-year-old boys to take out a lot of toys due to the nature of the way they were pretending. What a mistake! It was sheer agony for them to clean up, and I vowed not to repeat the scene.

The way children pretend has much to do with the way they will actually do things when they are older. If a young woman is cooking and continues to pull spices, flour, and other supplies off the shelf while baking, the mess at the end will be great. If instead she puts ingredients back in the cabinet as she uses them, cleanup will be manageable. If boys pull out all of the tools in the garage at once, the mess will be a big one. Using a few tools and then replacing them as they are finished will make the job much easier. Tasks such as picking up toys are much more than just for the sake of the tidiness of toys. Children are developing a positive habit regarding cleaning up their things that will go with them all through their life. By talking positively about cleaning up and maybe even singing some type of cleanup song, you can help your child develop a good attitude toward work at a very early age.

Serving one another in the home through work is a great model for serving Christ. I cannot stress enough how the right attitude affects the performance of our tasks. Even the most dismal of jobs can be done graciously if done with a right attitude. Sometimes the work that the Lord would have us do is difficult and stretches us beyond what we thought we could do. If as children we are taught proper attitudes toward service, we will be able to proceed even when the process is tough.

My little boys are a good example. Last summer the boys "helped" Jim as he cut wood for our wood-burning stove. What this means is that our five-year-old, Jimmy, stood by the log splitter and moved a lever whenever Jim gave him the go-ahead. While they worked Jim kept repeating the sentence, "We love to work." Pretty soon I heard the boys saying this often. One day they were outside in 104 degree heat working. Most little boys I know would be in a swimming pool on such a day. Not our Jimmy. He loves to work; so if Daddy is working, Jimmy wants to be working. They just kept drinking a lot of water and working.

It is not just in extreme heat that this is true. We have two rabbits and a seventy-five-pound Samoyed (dog) that live in our backyard. Every day they need to be fed. Even when it was 20 below zero last winter, my seven-year-old, Jenny, was out there feeding and watering them. She did not complain— she just did it.

Now is it always like this at my house? No way. My children do not always cheerfully serve each day. They do accept work as a natural part of their day, however. Many times I see their attitudes toward their tasks as being better than mine. I believe this to be a result of our positive approach to work. Jim and I work hard alongside the children. We do not expect more from them than we do from ourselves. We expect them to do what they are capable of at their age.

I have reviewed a few charts listing what tasks are appropriate for each age and have decided it is better to test each child. I find that when they are eager, they can do much more at an earlier age. Just recently we reshuffled our tasks in a way that gave Jimmy more responsibility. At five years old he is now feeding the animals, in addition to doing a few other things. He is thriving in these areas that I thought might be too hard for him. Jonathan at age three doesn't like to be left out and often accompanies Jimmy during the feeding of the animals. It is possible that Jonathan may be ready to feed the animals at age four. When Joanna was barely a year old, she insisted on helping unload the silverware from the dishwasher. With help she was encouraged to do so. Both Jamie and Jenny share much of the kitchen work. I pretty much do the cooking, and they do everything else. Lately they have been cooking entire meals too. In fact, in their eagerness they have asked me if they could do the whole meal without me. In my opinion, it doesn't get much better than this.

Part of our recent success with the younger boys' helping out more is a result of setting up teams. Two teams are assigned to various tasks. The nine-year-old works with the three-year-old, and the seven-year-old works with the five-year-old. Each team made up a name for themselves. Whenever the boys are wandering around after meals (this happens often), I send them back to their team leader for direction. The boys respond well to this approach and have complied so far without complaining. The girls have been able to train them properly and offer assistance when the new task is too great. It also helps to have some unassigned tasks that everybody pitches in to finish. This helps reduce comments such as "It's not my job." The statement that many hands make light work is true.

It depends on where you are starting with your children as to how much they can do at first. If you have older children who have not worked much in the home, work first on developing positive attitudes toward service. These attitudes do not develop as a result of paying them to do tasks. Our service to the Lord is done as service, not work for wages. We serve the Lord out of love, not because we are expecting something in return. I think it is important to be very careful to keep money separate from service in the home. If children link payment to tasks performed, they are missing out on some very good training in serving the Lord.

While it is common practice to give an allowance that is tied to completing certain tasks throughout a given week, I believe there is a better way. We provide for our children's needs, and when they are old enough to benefit from having money, we give them some periodically. It is very easy for a child to learn to work for money. It is not so easy to learn to work for nothing—to just want to serve. We want to be sure they learn to serve joyfully first; there will be plenty of time later to work for money. At age nine Jamie had already come up with some money-making ideas because of what she has done in our home.

While all of this may sound good to you, it doesn't just happen. Although we began with the right philosophy, we have had our share of difficulties in implementation. One of our problem areas involves defining what each person's service will be. It is not enough to request that a child do the dishes and clean up the counters. It is essential to set standards for each task so the child knows what is involved. In my mind, cleaning up the counters includes cleaning up the stove top, but unless I communicate this to my child, he or she won't know it. Even if you tell the child all that he or she needs to know about a certain task, he or she will probably forget. Other children who take over this task will also need to know.

We have decided to make up a card for each service that we request our children to perform. These are located in a small box for easy access to the children. Younger children can have the card read to them as they take on new responsibilities. These cards can be laminated and should last a long time. I have seen cards like this with organizer systems, but their standards never match up with what you expect in your own home. I suggest beginning to work on these cards when your children are small, so the cards will be ready to use when they are older.

A word of caution is in order regarding standards. They should not become an end in and of themselves. The process of learning how to do a task well is important. Diligence and perseverance are taught through this approach. Don't expect your child to master a new task after performing it once or twice. If he does, he needs more challenging work. At times I get frustrated with my older children because I feel they have been working on a particular task long enough to be proficient at it. I have to remember that some of the things they do are advanced beyond their years, and it is unreasonable to expect them to be as good at it as I am. The process of improving their performance over time is more important than having a perfectly executed task. We don't strive for perfection anyway. Perfection should be reserved only for those times that really need it. I speak as a retired perfectionist. Perfectionism only leads to burnout. It is better to find out what is adequate and do just that.

Communicating your expectations to your children is vital. Sometimes they have no idea how well I am expecting them to complete a task. If I fail in this area, they usually do less than I was expecting. We allow feedback from our children if they are struggling with our expectations. It is difficult to know if I am asking them to do something that is too much for them. I prefer to err by expecting too much than to give them too little to do. Allowing them to share their frustrations gives me a chance to make a change if needed before bad attitudes develop. If upon examination it is found that the child should be capable of what I am asking, he is required to do the task.

Probably my biggest stumbling block in this whole process is follow-up. The manager in me would like to delegate the work and then go do something else myself. No matter how competent my kids are, I have to keep reminding myself they are still children. They need follow-up! It is foolish to give directions and then expect those directions to be followed with little or no supervision or evaluation. It is just as bad to assume that children won't complete their work unless constantly reminded. Neither of these extremes works well. After children have completed their work, it is important that you inspect it. At this time you can point out areas that need improvement, and over time they will get it right. (You can also praise them for what they have done well.) Part of the reason my girls aren't as proficient at kitchen cleanup as I think they should be is that I have failed to inspect their work consistently enough to correct it where needed.

It doesn't have to be a nightmare to track all of these tasks and know who is supposed to do them and when. You can make up your own charts or purchase one of the organizing systems that are available. The best system that I have seen is PEGS system (Practical Encouragement and Guidance Systems). You can get more information on this from Family Tools, Inc. (612-717-0644).

We have used the PEGS for a number of years. Because of its flexibility and reusability, we have been able to change the way we implement it as our family needs change. The book that goes along with the system is an important tool to help you begin to organize all this information. I encourage you to check out this system!

Another tool I would recommend to help your family is available from Doorposts, P.O. Box 1610, Clackamas, OR 97015. This includes an "If-Then" chart that lists a negative behavior, attitude, or character quality on the left side, an appropriate Bible verse in the middle, and on the right a blank space to write down a consequence for exhibiting the inappropriate behavior. Conversely, there is a "Blessing" chart that lists positive qualities on the left side, an appropriate Bible verse in the middle, and a blank space on the right side for writing in a reward. These are poster-size and can be mounted on the wall for easy viewing for everyone.

Whatever system you use or design to track responsibilities, remember that it must be easy for you to use. Consistency is the key to success, and you won't be able to keep up with your charts if they are not convenient for you. It is a good idea to see how the children feel about a particular system. In our family, the system works best when the children are the ones who put up stickers or turn over disks on our PEGS. I involve the children as much as possible in the process. Working together as a team is invaluable life training.

Another helpful tool is the use of a flow chart. My neighbor, Karen, developed this approach one day as she realized that her four children kept asking her the same questions over and over. She devised a flow chart for the children to follow that answered typical questions such as "Can I start my schoolwork? Can I start my chores? Can I start my exercise? Can I enjoy leisure time (games, crafts, reading, play)? Can I read in bed?" I have included a modified sample of this chart in Appendix A. There are so many benefits to this approach that I would like to set up our own to meet our individual needs. I especially like the independent nature of this arrangement. Instead of Mom having to evaluate the same questions over and over, there are standard answers for routine questions. This helps keep your children on track without requiring you to repeat yourself. This frees Mom up for more important questions and teaches the children how to solve some of their problems on their own.

Now that you are better equipped to involve your children in the work that needs to be done in your home, let's talk about cleaning. Just mentioning the word *cleaning* sends many moms running the other direction. I think this is due in part to the fact that sometimes our homes are in such a seemingly hopeless condition that we don't see how we can possibly clean them. The key here is the word *seemingly*. No matter how bad your house may be at this very moment, there is hope! It may take some time, but once your home is in order, there are ways to keep it in good order that don't demand unlimited time.

Cleaning isn't really possible until you declutter. When we first began to home school, I had three children under five years old. To lighten my load as we were getting started, we decided to have someone come in to clean our home. I was shocked at how much cleaning I had to do before the cleaning person came. The clutter had to be processed by me. Once that was done, there wasn't much left to do. We only had the woman come twice before I realized that I could do the cleaning if I just kept the clutter under control. This is much easier said than done.

We have since designed built-in opportunities to declutter. I have ladies into my home once a month for a time of fellowship and teaching the topics in this book. This gives me a monthly opportunity to keep my living room free of clutter such as paper, magazines, and anything that we put up high so the baby can't get it. I am very busy with my six children, and it is easy for me to put something on a shelf and never get back to it. The activity level is so high in my family that I can literally walk by this type of clutter for months and not even see it.

We have a biannual, whole-house, deep clean that serves to keep clutter on the way out of our house. I am considering doing this quarterly to further minimize the amount of stuff we accumulate. In the spring, the excess we uncover from this deep clean becomes our annual garage sale. You may be thinking that clutter is useless stuff or stacks of old newspapers. While this is true, it is much more. Clutter is made up of good and useful things that no longer have utility for you.

I love books. As I pondered our full bookshelves, it occurred to me that many good books are only going to be read once. Many of these are not necessarily something I would be giving to my children later on. I went through our shelves and pulled off enough for one box of books to sell at the garage sale. They were books I would not be needing to refer to again. It was really freeing to see some open space on the shelf. It is also a good feeling to know that others will benefit from reading these books instead of just letting them collect dust. Another option I have exercised in the past when I am finished with books or decide that we don't want them is to donate them to a church library.

It really helps to have an outlet in mind where you can give things away. Garage sales are a great way to get rid of things, but I do not want to store everything for a once-a-year sale. Throughout the year, there are many charitable organizations that will gladly take your things off your hands. In our area I have been noticing people advertising in the local newspaper about giving things away free (big items such as swing sets and dining room sets). With a little creativity, you can find an outlet for your unwanted items.

Be careful, though, of becoming an outlet for other people's unwanted items. Because we let people know what we need, we are finding that from time to time people will give us things. This is great, and we appreciate it very much. Just be careful to keep only what you can use, and pass along the rest.

Once you get through the deep cleaning process, it is a good idea to organize your home if you have not already done so. Emilie Barnes has written a book entitled *Emilie's Creative Home Organizer* that deals specifically with how to do this in each area of your home. Once your home is organized to suit your needs, live in a way that minimizes clutter.

Paper is a problem for most of us. Try to just process it one time. I look through the mail and weed out the junk before sorting my mail from my husband's and sometimes letters for our children. My husband's mail goes into a folder marked "mail," and I am done with it. He knows where to find the mail, and I don't have to be concerned about little ones playing post office and relocating Daddy's mail. I put my mail on my pillow so that hopefully I will be able to process it before retiring that evening. If time does not permit, I put it on my desk.

My desk is an interesting topic at our house. I would prefer it to be an office, but it is only a desk. It holds folders with outlines of chapters for this book, catalogs for me to read in preparation for the next school year, a couple of games that I made for our school that still need to be laminated, copies of science worksheets for three children for next year that still need to be filed in their notebooks, other assorted "important" papers, and a box of Kleenex. There are a few more things on the floor by my desk chair. Jim politely asked me the other day to pile it more neatly so he could safely get to the telephone. I guess you get the picture. As organized as I am, my desk is a mess. In surveying other women I found that every single one of them has a desk that is a mess too.

I tell you this as an encouragement. I used to think that I could keep up with my desk. I can see now that due to the sheer volume of work represented by the pile on the desk and the finite resource of my own energy, I will have some degree of clutter on my desk at this stage of my life. There are times when it is very neat—such as when I am cleaning it. I suggest letting a desk go for no more than six weeks or you may never want to touch it. For me, this level of clutter on a finite space (the desk) works. I can find what I need pretty easily in most cases. I wish it were neater, but this is one hurdle I haven't been able to jump yet.

Probably the best anti-clutter lifestyle change we have made is to have a finite space for items. One example is our use of eighteen-gallon Rubbermaid containers to store clothing that is not being used. Containers have labels indicating whether the clothes are for a boy or a girl and the appropriate size. Clothing that works for either a boy or a girl (primarily newborn and infant clothing) is located in whatever container holds clothing for our last child. If I get anything new, I must get rid of something old so the lid will fit on. I am limited by the space in the container, which provides ample clothing for that particular size as I have set it up. I also have one eighteen-gallon Rubbermaid container for each child. In it I store their baby calendar, first pair of shoes, and other special things. They may save things too, but with the reminder that when they grow up and leave our home, all of their treasures must fit in the container. This helps them to evaluate which papers are important and to begin to minimize clutter while they are young. It also makes this a more simple process than hauling away box after box of things that you throw away anyway once you go through them. Our girls will also have a hope chest in which to store items they are making for their future homes.

I have a box rule for current "treasures" for each child. They each have a box (this could be a smaller Rubbermaid container or a cardboard box with lid from the produce section of the super-market) in their room that must hold all of their "stuff." If the box is full, they can't get anything new until they get rid of something. Stationery, notes, knickknacks, etc. all fall under this category. The boys have different types of things in their boxes, but they have a finite space for the stuff just the same. This method has revolu-tionized bedroom cleaning. Since the children aren't allowed to accumulate much, they have little to clean up. This is a blessing to them in many ways. It helps them weed out their stuff periodically while still allowing them to accumulate "treasures." It develops a clutter-free environment and the means to keep it that way. By making this a habit as a child, hopefully they will have better con-trol over clutter in their future homes than we do.

Beyond their boxes, we limit just how much we allow in their bedrooms. We have a corporate location for books, games, and craft supplies. Our girls have sewing machines, but their supplies and machines are not in their bedrooms. We use our bedrooms for sleeping and have the children play elsewhere in our home. This way there really is very little to clean up in a bedroom even when it gets messy. Having toys and other items located in a corporate location (perhaps a family room) encourages the entire family to help clean up, which makes the task much easier. We do not provide shelves of any kind in children's bedrooms. I remember as a child that I had three long shelves that stretched across an entire wall of my bedroom. I had "stuff" on every shelf. It was a terrible mess, and even after I had finished cleaning it, there was an untidy appearance. We have shelves in the living areas of our home that stay relatively tidy as a part of daily cleanup.

A final help in keeping bedrooms tidy is the concept of a morning and evening room check. I learned this concept through using my PEGS. Inspecting a bedroom at the beginning and again at the end of the day minimizes just how messed up it can become. Most of the time my children can make their rooms tidy in less than five minutes using this technique. When I have strayed from this process, I have discovered some pretty big messes.

The finite space we give for papers is a clear plastic wall unit located in the living room. It has three sections that hold standard-size file folders. In my section I have a magazine that I am reading, my clipboard (more about that in the next chapter), and assorted odds and ends. My husband has file folders for mail, maintenance needed around the home, and questions the children have for him. If he is not home when something comes up, we simply leave a note in the appropriate folder. The third section holds a written copy of our daily schedule and other information pertinent to the children's service for that week.

We have even instituted a finite space rule for children's school books and work. Each child has a plastic crate to store his or her supplies. They all have a pencil case that belongs in their crate. Every once in a while the crate is too full and sloppy. They then have to clean it out so everything fits well. If they want to go work somewhere else in the house, they just pick up their crate and everything they need is right there. I require them to keep books they are reading in their crates unless they actually have them in their hands and are reading them. Otherwise I find books all over the house that the children are reading, and sometimes they are unable to locate them. By requiring them to put books back into their crates, they will know where to find the books when they want to pick them up again.

By now you may be feeling that you play a pretty big role in following up and inspecting. It is true, you do. But this preventative approach to clutter is far simpler and takes much less time than always trying to dig out from a house that is buried two feet deep in "stuff." Once you have the children's clutter under control, there are just a few more things you must do.

Keep newspapers going out into the recycling as fast as they come in. You should only have today's paper in the house. Tear out articles you don't have time to read, or pitch the whole paper if you don't get to it. Papers pile up faster than anything, and rarely can you ever catch up on the days you did not get to read. Be prudent about selecting which books you wish to own. Public and church libraries offer many titles. Utilize the cookbooks that can be found in the library. I find copying recipes at the library to be a good "mom alone" activity at the end of a busy day.

What is left to do after all of the clutter is gone? Not much unless you are striving for a home that could be in *Better Homes and Gardens*. Jim says that if his house could be featured in *Better Shacks and Sheds*, he would be happy. I confess that I don't really like to clean my house. We certainly keep it livable, but the idea of investing so much time in cleaning what will become dirty so quickly (you should see how long my floor stays clean) turns me off. I believe that most of my time should be spent on things with eternal value. Colossians 3:2 says, "Set your minds on things above, not on earthly things." My time, talents, and energy are spent primarily on my children. They have eternal value. At our house we minimize our cleaning as much as possible. Cleaning the bathrooms and kitchen, vacuuming, and dusting pretty much sums it up. We do bigger jobs such as washing windows only as needed.

My advice to the working mother is to pay someone to clean your home. Even if it is twice a month or just once a month, it will help a lot. Your time is limited, and your children need you. Home-schooling mothers benefit from the energies of their children. Learn to harness that energy, and have them do most of the cleaning. They will know how to do it well by the time they leave your home. If you are the mother of preschoolers, I suggest that you relax your standards. The children will grow quickly, and the physical demands on you won't be so great. The physical demands of keeping a spotless house while curious toddlers work against your efforts is just too much. Enjoy your little ones!

I want to mention two books that will help you declutter and then clean what is left. *Clutter's Last Stand* by Don Aslett is a humorous look at what to do about all of your clutter. This book is a real motivator for those of you who are hesitant about getting started. *Clean and Green* by Annie Berthold-Bond is a book that shares almost 500 ways to clean with products that are non-toxic. Many of them you can make yourself with products you already have around the home, such as Borax and baking soda. The book emphasizes being environmentally safe, and I find its strength to be the safety of the cleaning agents for my children to use. I have never been fond of the harsh chemicals found in typical cleaning supplies. This book lists products that are safe to use and tells you where to find them.

Laundry

I have saved the best for last. Many women groan when I mention laundry. I suspect that laundry can be one of the most irritating aspects of homemaking if it is not kept under control.

Laundry never stops, and it is a rather mundane task that is easy to put off. There are ways to make it easier on yourself. Let's explore some of these.

I only wash once a week for a family of seven. I do this because I don't like having dirty and clean laundry lying around every day of the week. I have no desire to interact with my laundry any more frequently than once a week. I don't really have that many loads. We have a large capacity washer, and I wash about six loads of clothing (not including diapers, towels, or sheets) per week. We wear our clothes for more than one day if possible. Denim works well for two or three days if you just change your shirt. In the summer months, my boys usually go through a pair of jeans per day, but that is not all year long. I also see no reason why they can't wear yesterday's jeans with mud on them if they are heading out to the yard to get dirty again.

I have small square laundry baskets for each child to carry their own clean clothes to their room and put away by themselves as soon as they are able. The empty baskets are stored in their closets as a place for them to put dirty clothes. I use these small baskets to sort the laundry on laundry day. I encourage all of the children to help. They can sort at an early age, and utilizing them in laundry sorting helps them learn to classify. They need to understand the difference between darks and whites and which clothes are in between. Even Joanna at age one was very interested in the process. She doesn't sort well, but we are reinforcing her desire to learn.

There are time-savers that make laundry go faster. We sort the clothes the night before laundry day. I put the denim/dark load in the washer before going to bed. This load usually takes the longest to dry. If I am up to use the bathroom or am nursing a baby in the middle of the night, I throw the load in the dryer and start another load. When I wake up in the morning, I already have one load dry (the folding of this load goes fast) and another ready to go in the dryer. I try to take clothes out of the dryer as soon as it beeps, so wrinkles are minimized and I don't have much ironing. Even if I can't fold right that minute, I can lay out the clothes. I usually fold our laundry in a central location such as the living room. This way I can go back and forth to the kitchen and also maximize the assistance of family members who are passing through the living room. It is amazing how quickly laundry can be folded with everyone taking a turn at folding some of the clothes. I have plastic hangers (the kind that hold infant and toddler clothes) for each girl, and we use clothespins to hang tights or my nylons on the appropriate hanger in the bathroom. Once they are dry, the owner must put their own things away unless they are too young.

Once all of the laundry is finished, the older children take their baskets to their rooms and put their clean clothes away. I put away the rest. At times I will have to leave this part until the next day, but then I make sure I finish the task. As I train my children in task completion, it is important for me to model this for them in the way I complete my own tasks.

As warmer weather returns I am reminded of my clothesline. I did not think I would like this at first. Clotheslines seemed like more work to me, and I am not looking for more work. After I tried one, I was pleasantly surprised. We can hang up two or three loads at once. This is faster because the dryer is much slower than the washer. I can be outside enjoying nice weather while conversing with my children. They often offer to help, and even the little ones can hand me the clothespins. I have noticed that denim dried on the line often does not need ironing.

There are a few things I don't hang on the line. I prefer to dry our undergarments in the dryer. I dry cloth diapers in the dryer too since I don't like the way they come out on the line.

My approach to laundry may not work for your situation, so I am including different methods that others have used successfully. I know of a family with ten children who has the children in each bedroom do the laundry for that room. The oldest child in the room is responsible for the process. Another family lines up three laundry baskets in the laundry room. Each night a child is assigned to gather all of the laundry for that day and sort it into darks, whites, and coloreds. When the baskets are full, they do the laundry. A friend of mine with seven children prefers to have a children's laundry basket located in a central location in the hallway.

No matter how you do your laundry, it is important to keep up with it. Laundry, like clutter, is manageable if you stay current. If you allow it to pile up, it becomes a monster too big to tame. For some of you this chapter may have really put you on edge. You may already have the clutter and laundry monsters living at your house. Be encouraged by starting out small. You didn't create the mess in one day, and it will take longer than that to clean it up. But once you do get things under control, the next chapter will help you keep your home functioning smoothly from day to day.

8

Organizing for Smooth Household Management

IT IS NOT ENOUGH TO GET YOUR HOME IN GOOD ORDER. WITH-out a plan to keep it that way, you will find yourself falling back into old patterns quickly. It takes effort to keep our homes running smoothly. But with a little planning and forethought as to how you work best, it can be done. First we need to define what an orderly home will be for your family.

A verse we have posted in our kitchen is 1 Corinthians 14:40, "But everything should be done in a fitting and orderly way." God is a God of order. While we will never attain perfection, it should be our goal to become more orderly in our daily living. This is pleasing to God. Earlier in the same chapter, Paul is referring to order in the church when he says, "For God is not a God of disorder but of peace" (v. 33). I know that when things get out of control at my house, I feel anything but peace. I believe these words of wisdom for the church are applicable to our homes.

Just how to go about organizing your daily life will depend largely upon how you function. Books on organizing tend to enhance the lives of people who already have a natural inclination toward being organized. Some of us just know how to pull it all together and keep it running smoothly. Others of us cannot make it work even with the help of the best resources on organizing. This is true because we don't all look at things from the same perspective.

I learned this truth the hard way while Jim was home for four months after surgery for a work-related injury. I enthusiastically looked forward to his days at home with us. He had gone through surgery on his knee, and although he had not healed enough to return to firefighting, he could walk and function around the home. I figured that with another adult around, my daily schedule would hum like our honeybees. Boy, was I wrong! Jim thinks completely differently than I do. (This is more than just male and female differences.) With my carefully organized daily structure complete with specific mealtimes, I thought he would just jump on the program with us. What I found was that he could not function well in such a structured environment. He detested my time-oriented schedules and my own method of organization. While he operates in a completely different mode than I do, he gets much done. It was at this time that I decided to learn more about right- and left-brain orientation.

Organizing for the Creative Person by Dorothy Lehmkuhl and Dolores Cotter Lamping addresses these issues. If you can overlook introductory remarks that focus on relying on self and inner strength to get you going, there is a wealth of helpful information here. They explain right- and left-brain orientation or dominance in such a way that it is readily understandable. Each of us uses both sides of our brain, but we tend to function more dominantly in one side or the other. This affects us dramatically. "While the right brain produces a broad spectrum of intuitive and creative talents, the left brain produces those talents necessary for traditional organizing skills. It's only natural, then, that people who prefer right-brain activities will have developed more right-brain skills and may not have concentrated their efforts as much on learning left-brain organizing skills."[1]

You may have guessed it. I function happily in my left brain, while my husband thrives in his right brain. This does not make one of us better than the other, but it does mean we organize differently. Both of us have inherent pros and cons in the way we work. Jim often forgets where he has placed something or what he was supposed to do if it is not written down. I, on the other hand, tend to get flustered if our daily structure gets too casual. I find this stressful. If plans change greatly for a given day, Jim acclimates much easier and can readily go with the flow. I share this with you to illustrate that it is neither all bad or all good in either area of brain dominance. What is important is to know your weaknesses and deal with them. Even if you function predominantly in your right brain, you can learn to be organized.

We need to get an idea of the traits associated with each brain dominance. We can then begin to show how to develop skills even if they don't come naturally. The authors of *Organizing for the Creative Person* refer to right-brain orientation as "Arbie" and left-brain orientation as "Elbie." A few of the characteristics of an "Elbie" (that's me) include being detail-oriented, very aware of time, and thriving with structure. An "Arbie" (that's Jim) tends to be oblivious to time, has a global approach (big picture), and is a laid-back type of person. Those who naturally tend toward being organized pay attention to time management, prioritizing, and developing a comfortable structure for the home. If this is not a description of you, I suggest you buy their book and benefit from their "right-brain styles for conquering clutter, mastering time, and reaching your goals."[2]

For further help if you are one who tends toward disorganization, I highly recommend reading some of Sandra Felton's materials. She has authored many books that help disorganized people pull it all together. She publishes a newsletter called *Messies Anonymous* that will help you in more ways than I can. Contact her at 5025 S.W. 114th Avenue, Miami, FL 33165; phone: 305-271-8404. Her credentials, given on the back of her book *The*

Messies Manual, are as follows: "Sandra Felton knows what it's like to slap a 'quarantined' sign on the front door and hide when the deacons call unexpectedly. Because she is a teacher (who only grades papers she can find) and the mother of three, she understands the problems of a busy woman who has to keep the house clean. This reformed Messie founded Messies Anonymous in 1980 and has taught the 'how-to's' of good housekeeping to hundreds of disorganized people."[3]

In setting up your own system of organizing your day, there are some helpful questions to ask first. What takes up more of my time than it should (for example, meal planning and preparation or getting dressed in the morning)? What time restrictions am I forced to work around (for example, your husband's work hours, your own work hours, school hours, etc.)? Who is available to help me? What is their skill level? Are they "Elbies" or "Arbies"? What aspects of household management are least appealing to me (for example, cleaning)? It may be best to write down your responses to these questions and discuss them with the entire family. Take time for reflection on your answers. You may find areas that need a major overhaul while others need only a little fine tuning.

I have made changes pretty much on an ongoing basis as our family continues to grow. Some of these changes are rather simple. Long ago I abandoned my shower at the beginning of the day. There just isn't time for me to do this when I need to be directing my family during the morning rush hour. (Even though we home school and don't leave the house, we still have morning rush hour.) I take my shower at night before I go to bed to simplify my morning grooming routine. I have a simple hairstyle of long hair that gets pulled back or put in a ponytail. My jumpers and T-shirts are simple to put on, so my entire morning routine can be executed in a matter of minutes.

Recently I have had to wait to read the mail until after the children are in bed. I love getting the mail. Usually I would drop whatever I was doing to read the mail as soon as it came. Time does not permit this anymore, and after a cursory glance I usually put it on my pillow to be read before I go to bed.

These two examples may seem to be small issues, but small issues add up to hours in your day. There may be some activities in your home you could group together to save time. While you are in your kitchen, take a minute to jot down items needed at the grocery store. As much as possible, do more than one thing while you are in a room. When you go to the bathroom, straighten the towel that is crumpled before leaving. Pick up stray papers in the living room as you pass through. Pretty soon you will see how little time it takes to keep organized if you do a little here and a little there.

Our family system of organization is still in transition. We have many systems that work, while others need modification. I hope our story will be an encouragement to you since we are blending two adults—a "cleanie" and a "messie" (to borrow Sandra Felton's terminology). Over the years I have observed that I am becoming more disorganized (remember my desk?) and Jim is becoming more organized. This is good for harmony in the home. Keep in mind that organization may not come naturally for all of your children. Keeping your organizational structure balanced for your own family's needs is the key to success.

Since I primarily run our home on a daily basis, I need to be comfortable with our structure. We have a saying in our home: "Mom needs a track to run on." During the time Jim was off work, we did not always have this. Jimmy was four years old at the time and often included a request in his prayers that we would "get back on track." I don't function well without some type of outline for the week. Jim prefers only to know what needs to happen daily. Some type of plan is essential to a smoothly functioning home. Be it daily or weekly, make sure you have a plan.

Before I share the nuts and bolts of my method, I want to stress the importance of complementing each other. Be it husband/wife or mother/children, we must share our strengths and help in our weak areas. As the more structured person, I try to help Jim identify what is most important for each day. He works hard and accomplishes much by starting on the most important tasks first. Prioritizing is difficult for him but comes naturally to me. In a supportive way, I use my strength to offset his weak area. Certainly this is one thing God intended for wives to do. In Genesis 2:18 we read, "The LORD God said, 'It is not good for the man to be alone. I will make a helper suitable for him.'" Even if your husband is at work all day, you can be a help to him. Jim helps me in my weak areas too. It is hard to admit, but I have a tendency to be too serious and driven, so he reminds me to kick back and relax.

One of the best tools I have used to keep organized is a clipboard. Mine is 8 1/2 x 11" and holds my most important papers (the rest are on my desk). The first page is my weekly menu plan. Everyone in the family knows that the menu plan is on the clipboard, and many times I have found that several aspects of a meal have been started because others knew what needed to be done. My seven-year-old, Jenny, refers to this plan often. It is interesting to note that her organizing style is much like my own. Underneath the menu plan I clip small papers, such as a list of purchases I want to make at garage sales this season, shopping lists, clothing needs for the children, and currently two coupons for free bowling for my daughters. If I am going out, I know at a glance what items we need. When I don't use this system faithfully, I always forget what I need.

The next page is an ongoing "to do" list. At the top of the page I list small, manageable items. At the bottom I list projects that I will need to set aside a day or two to complete. Right now I have two such projects listed. The first is to reorganize my cookbook into three binders. This project is what we call a "sitter subject." It has been sitting on my list for months. I can't seem to get to it, so this summer I will set aside specific time to work on it. The other project is to go through my files and get rid of anything I don't need anymore. This is another project I can't seem to finish. I decided to let nine-year-old Jamie help me by going through all our curriculum catalogs and weeding out the old ones. I will look at it before getting rid of anything, but the process will go much faster with her sorting it for me. This is a good habit for her to learn anyway. Use your children in the organizing process! It is good for all of you.

The next page is a worksheet of information I put together the last time I did quantity cooking. I will probably prepare a number of meals before our baby is born (since this writing, our child has arrived), and I will refer to this sheet at that time. The next page is a list of the bulk produce for this year including price, date, and location of purchase. The next page is last year's list, which will help me remember when and where we found the best prices for the things we bought last year. The final page on my clipboard is a phone list for MOPs (Mothers of Preschoolers).

Your clipboard can contain anything you want. I like it because it is a finite space that naturally controls how much paper clutter it will hold. It is easy to take along in the car. If you are traveling anywhere and someone else is driving, you can quickly review the lists in your clipboard to see if something needs to be changed. I sometimes forget what I have on my clipboard and can easily get back on track with a quick look. I confess that there have been weeks at a time where I have not used my clipboard. During this time I have made multiple trips to the grocery store for just a few items, been ill-prepared at mealtime, totally forgotten some important items that needed my attention, and so on. I rely on my clipboard to stay organized. Try this out on your children. I purchased small clipboards that hold smaller-sized paper for my girls to use to keep themselves in order. Neither one of them uses it faithfully, but they both have benefited at different times from using this system.

There are various ways that you can successfully work

through each day. For me, due to the sheer volume of activity daily, I prefer to have a pretty detailed outline for the day. As I have said, this desire is not shared by all family members. I must take this into account if I want my home to run smoothly. Here is what we have done:

I have written out our schedule so it can be referred to as needed. Parts of this schedule apply up until 9 A.M. daily, while the rest of it pertains to three days per week for the sake of our school. Here is what our schedule looks like:

7:00 A.M.	Mom and Dad get up
7:15	Kids get up
7:30	Morning grooming completed
7:45	Morning room check
7:45 - 8:00	Feed animals, get breakfast ready
8:00 - 8:45	Breakfast and cleanup
8:45 - 9:00	Independent devotional time for everyone
9:00 - 9:15	Bible tape
9:15 - 11:00	Formal structured family school time
11:00 - 11:30	Mom walks (when Dad is home), girls get lunch ready
11:30 - 12:30	Lunch and cleanup (including toys)
12:30 - 1:30	Piano practice for the girls
1:30 - 3:00	Meal preparation, sewing, crafts, learning games, independent assignments
3:00 - 3:30	Read to the younger children
3:30 - 5:00	Free time if all service (chores) are done
5:00 - 6:00	Dinner and cleanup
6:00 - 7:00	Baths (not every night) and get ready for bed

7:00	Bed for children under five years old
7:00 - 8:00	Reading/sewing time for older children
8:00	Lights out for all children (unless permission is granted for reading in bed for another half hour)

Before you groan at the apparent severity of such a schedule, rest assured that I have not been able to make this work consistently. On the days that do flow well, my children are thrilled with the amount of free time they have and the sense of accomplishment they feel. I did not intend for us to follow this schedule to the letter. It is a target to shoot for in our day-to-day living. The rigid time slots are set to keep us from spending too much time on some tasks, leaving no time for other tasks. Mealtime in particular can drag on without a restriction on how long you wish to spend on the meal. Since we spend all day together, we often curtail talking by the children at mealtime until they are finished. This shortens the time we spend for meals.

Do not be impressed by the balance of activities represented by the schedule. Sewing, crafts, and reading to the younger children during the time allotted rarely happen. My daily walks are not yet done regularly. Our family is in process, just as your family is right now. We see improvements from year to year, and you do too. By having some type of schedule listed in writing, you make it easier on yourself to see areas of improvement. What never seems to get done is also painfully obvious, even though it is on your schedule.

It is not necessary to be as detailed as I am in the schedule. My husband cannot function with so much detail. Conversely, I cannot function without some type of schedule (a track to run on). A compromise between these two extremes is a checkpoint system. Rather than having an entire day outlined, you simply establish checkpoints along the way. This could be getting up and going to bed at the same time each day. Plan your mealtimes (all three of them) to be at regular times if at all possible. I understand that in our culture this is almost impossible for some families. That is why we have chosen to simplify our life, decrease our income and working hours outside the home, and limit the activities our children participate in that conflict with our meals. On the days when Jim is not at the firehouse, we have three sitdown family meals per day. We maintain this because we feel it is important for the family to come together at these times. Other checkpoints may include music practice at the same time each day to make it a habit. Opportunities for daily/weekly chores should be done before free time. By using a checkpoint system, you still have an outline for your day; but rather than being based on specific times, you are following a pattern of "what comes next?"

I prefer my own schedule, but Jim functions well with a checkpoint system. When he is at work, we may choose to adhere pretty strictly to my schedule. This is particularly true if we are trying to accomplish a lot in one day. When Jim is home, we relax the structure a bit. We still try to follow my plan, but he is only aware of selected checkpoints in my plan (time to get up and mealtimes). I have seen us all flourish with this type of structured flexibility. It is good for your children to learn to function in a changing environment while they are young. By organizing in this manner, we are finding that our children are discovering how they like to organize the best. If you are less organized than your children (this does happen), then by all means let them have the option of designing a schedule that works for them. I rely on Jamie all the time to help me remember things that I forget. I'm sure those of you with children in school would benefit from your children keeping you informed as to when and where they need to be picked up.

As you can see, we have had to do some experimenting with scheduling at our house. Even though we have less outside commitments than many (meetings, sports activities, clubs, etc.), we still find it imperative to have a plan for our days if we are to accomplish our goals. It is probable that you will have to try different methods or adapt something to fit your own family. Respect other family members' discomfort if they have trouble with your schedule or plan. You may need to adjust something for one or two people because of the way they are made up. Remember, Jim is very productive. He just goes about it in an entirely different way than I do. That is okay. God never intended us to all be the same.

There are some forms and charts that our family finds useful in the organizing process. I love our dry-erase weekly planner that we keep on our refrigerator. We have used this for years, and it works great! I color code our activities by the person doing them. I write family activities in black, my activities in blue, Jim's in green, and the children's in red. I put an X on the evenings when Jim will be working. It is easy to see if we are overbooking for a week and need to decline to commit ourselves any further. I generally list "make bread" on one day and "laundry" on another for myself. There also was a time where I picked out at least two days per week to "stay home." Living in the suburbs, it is too tempting to run out for something every day since everything is so convenient. If you don't stay home, it is difficult to do a good job at homemaking. By using my calendar to plan to stay at home, I have developed the habit so that I no longer need to write it down.

It is a good idea to get a grip on the week by Sunday evening at the latest. I plan meals around the activities that are planned for the week and also make decisions regarding whether or not we are totally booked for the week. It takes conscious effort to keep the pace slower in the "fast lane" where we live. Additionally, I have found that if you want to get together with another family, it is best to ask at least a week in advance because chances are that their calendar is already full.

Both Jim and I use a daily planner/calendar that we compare frequently. If it is not on my calendar, it does not exist for me. It is important to make sure other family members let you know if they put something on their calendar so you do not have two things scheduled at the same time. I use my own planner when I put up our family weekly planner on the refrigerator. If I have missed anything, it is usually detected that day as everyone sees the week at a glance.

I have mentioned my weekly menu plan a few times already, but I want you to know what happens when I don't use it. It often costs us money. If I don't plan for us to use up leftovers in a timely fashion, they end up being thrown out as spoiled food. I may end up with an unbalanced meal if I haven't planned ahead. The most costly of all is having to go out to eat because it is dinnertime and nothing has been made for dinner. To me, this is the ultimate waste of money. If you plan to go out to eat, that is fine. But eating out due to a failure to plan dinner is expensive.

The PEGS chart (Practical Encouragement and Guidance system) that I introduced in the last chapter keeps the children on track with their responsibilities. When I don't use this system, they ask for it back. They like it because they know what to expect next during their day. They can also refer to my lists to know just what their daily and weekly responsibilities are without having to ask me. The key to success here is information. The children need to know what to do, when to do it, and how it should be done (see the previous chapter regarding the helpfulness of standard cards).

A very helpful chart that I have been keeping for a few years is my "harvest record." Since we buy produce in bulk when it is in season and then preserve it by canning, freezing, or dehydrating, I need to know how much we purchase and whether or not we finished it. Initially we just guessed how much of something to buy. When we had fifty gallons of apple cider pressed, I thought that was excessive—until the hot summer months came and we finished it all! I can refer to my "harvest record" and easily gauge the quantity to purchase. I also list *where* we purchase the produce. When we find a better source of something, we will know it since we can evaluate what we have done in previous years. This tool helps me greatly because I cannot remember these details from one year to the next.

Goal setting has been an opportunity for our family to become more organized. We initially set goals and objectives for each child as part of our home schooling, but we have since decided to expand this process. Although we have set goals for our home school, this is also appropriate for you to do for your children if they are in private or public school. Goal setting is much like setting up a daily schedule for your family. You need something to aim for in the training process.

We use a three-ring notebook to store all the objectives and year-end reports for all our children from year to year. I keep these together so I can refer back to different ages and see what I expected of each child. It is good to look through these from time to time to see just how well the children are doing. This is especially helpful on a day where things are not going smoothly.

In developing these goals, we use several categories—spiritual, academic, character, work skills, physical, and a life principle—that form our goals and objectives for each child. Here is an example of some of the things we expected from Jamie this year (fourth grade):

Spiritual	individual devotional/prayer time
Academic	proficiency in multiplication
Character	prompt obedience; follow directions after the first request
Work skills	task completion
Physical	have hair brushed by a parent daily (her hair is past her waist)
Life principle	love one another

There are many advantages to having goals and objectives for your children. It helps to keep you focused on what is most important for that year. Imagine if you tried to work on all of your own weaknesses all at once. This would be very discouraging. Goals and year-end evaluations help you see in writing the progress that occurs from year to year. This process also helps identify weak areas that may need extra help. It also gives your child a sense of accomplishment to see his or her growth, particularly in areas of spiritual and character growth that may not be noticed as easily by him or her. Your child also has a personal record of what was appropriate for him at each level. This will help him in training your grandchildren. Goal setting has been so successful for the children that we are now considering doing this for ourselves.

Books are readily available that offer scope and sequences to help guide you in setting academic goals. Two books I would recommend for this purpose are *Teaching Children—A Curriculum Guide to What Children Need to Know at Each Level Through Sixth Grade* by Diane Lopez, and *Curriculum Manual—Elementary Grades* by Cathy Duffy. If you use these books as guidelines and do not let yourself be overwhelmed by them, you should do well. Most other categories need to be set and evaluated by the parents for each individual child. Our objectives are personalized and are not exactly the same for each child at a given age.

A new planning strategy for our family is an "annual family goals/calendar." We have found that certain needs arise at about the same time each year. By documenting these, we would be better prepared as the inevitable comes up each year. Here is what we have come up with so far in the development process:

January/February	winter projects (this could be anything)
March	order seeds for the garden; spring cleaning; prepare for a new honeybee season (order bees if necessary)

March through June	review curriculum needs for next year; purchase books and supplies
April	clean up the yard; begin seed starts indoors
May	have our annual garage sale
June	pick strawberries; write up year-end reports for the children
July	pick blueberries
August	pick peaches; begin putting up the harvest
September	pick apples
Fall	Dad takes the children camping

This list is by no means complete, but it gives you an idea of what I am talking about. As we develop this idea further, we will be working toward a finished product that will make our lives easier. Currently we forget to do things and end up playing catch-up all the time. By outlining the typical activities and when they occur each year, we can be better prepared. The goals section of our calendar will keep us focused on a manageable amount of projects for the year.

I am stopping here so you will not be overwhelmed. If what I have shared so far is too much for you, consider looking into the books I recommended at the beginning of the chapter. These strategies come fairly naturally to me, but that does not mean they will for you. Adapt my ideas to fit your style. Remember that we did not start out doing all of these things at once. As I just indicated, the annual family calendar is being put together for the first time this year.

Households do not run smoothly by themselves. Left alone, households usually run wild. Manage your home in a way that is comfortable for you and your family. We have different personalities in our family that affect how we organize our home. This is true in your family too. Prepare to fail. Daily life ebbs and flows; so too will the smoothness of your household organization.

The first trimester of a pregnancy and the last month are times that my home does not function optimally. I don't feel well enough to keep up my organizational system. I suggest having an alternate "bare bones" plan for such times or when illness strikes. That way you will have realistic expectations of what you can accomplish while you are under the weather. After a slump time, go back to the plans you have designed for your family. If they don't work, modify them until they do. You are unique and special and know best how to apply the suggestions that will work best for you and your family.

Once your home is in order and you can keep it that way, you may be considering some of type of home business for yourself or your family. Some tips for this will be given in the next chapter.

9

Home
Business

IT MAY SEEM OUT OF PLACE TO PRESENT A CHAPTER ON THIS topic after I have discussed the many blessings that come from staying home to care for your family. The reason this has even come up is that through the writing of this book, I have found myself with a home business. Although I did not set out to establish a business at home, nevertheless I now have one that embodies all the pros and cons of working at home. I believe there are circumstances that lend themselves beautifully to women working out of their home. There are a few words of caution, however.

Those of you who are working full-time outside the home may be considering an option that is rapidly becoming a popular way to keep your job and stay at home at the same time. Companies are beginning to offer the option of bringing home your computer and doing your work from there. This saves time in commuting as well as saving in other ways. Commonly known as telecommuting, this option is not necessarily the answer for women who want to be at home. Consider for a moment your current office situation. If your children would sit quietly throughout your work day at the office, then it is likely that telecommuting will work for you. The reality is that once you are at home with your computer, the children will not likely be content to sit at your feet while you work all day. This may be an attractive situation for women with children who are all in school, but preschoolers do not thrive in this environment. It is almost worse for them, because you are there in front of them, but are essentially ignoring them while you work.

Instead, I would like to examine Scripture to lay a foundation of decision-making for the woman interested in working out of her home. Very early in the Bible we read about God's plan for the role of women. Although many in today's culture find fault with this, I believe God meant what he said. When he created a wife for Adam, "The LORD God said, 'It is not good for the man to be alone. I will make a helper suitable for him'" (Genesis 2:18). This verse does not say women should not work, but it does give us a priority. We are to be a helper suitable to our husband. There are a few husbands who thrive on the responsibilities of home-making. My own husband excels in the area of cleaning, and our family benefits from his help in this area. Overall, though, I believe that most husbands desire for the wife to care for the home. As much as Jim is a help to me, he does not want to be responsible for the running of the home. If this is the case, then we must assume that in order to be successful at working out of our home, we need to be capable at keeping our homes running smoothly in the process. This book has given you some tools to accomplish that goal.

A good example of a woman who worked at home and ran her home well is found in Proverbs 31. These verses are encouraging if we keep in mind that this woman was balanced and did not try to do everything all at once. Proverbs 31:10-31 describes her life overall, not just a single day in her life. These verses begin by talking about her relationship to her husband: "A wife of noble character who can find? She is worth far more than rubies. Her husband has full confidence in her and lacks nothing of value.

She brings him good, not harm, all the days of her life" (vv. 10-12). In establishing our businesses at home, we are bringing harm to our husbands and our families if we begin to let our home-making responsibilities slide.

There is a certain desk in my bedroom (mine of course) that currently has a pile eighteen inches high with my "work." Even though I can find what I need, this mess bothers Jim. He tells me about it often. As I finish writing this book, I am realizing that the delicate balance between working at our business and working on our responsibilities at home is hard to strike. When I am finished writing, I must reestablish the standards for my desk that suit Jim (and myself too!). Future writing or speaking engagements will have to be done in such a way that I have time to keep my desk in order.

The next three verses describe the woman's role in her home: "She selects wool and flax and works with eager hands. She is like the merchant ships, bringing food from afar. She gets up while it is still dark; she provides food for her family and portions for her servant girls" (vv. 13-15). I can relate to her desire to sew and provide healthy food for her family—and having to get up while it is still dark just to get it all done. I haven't yet run across any servant girls at my house. (Maybe my daughters fill this role.) So far in six verses we understand her relationship to her husband and some of her family responsibilities. Working out of the home has not yet been mentioned, but here it comes.

"She considers a field and buys it; out of her earnings she plants a vineyard. She sets about her work vigorously; her arms are strong for her tasks. She sees that her trading is profitable, and her lamp does not go out at night" (vv. 16-18). In addition to bringing good to her husband and caring for her family, this woman is able to manage a business. Note that even though she gets up while it is still dark, we read here that her light does not go out at night.

Becoming a good wife and maintaining this role, caring for

your family, *and* working out of your home is demanding. It will certainly be too much for some of us. Others may fail because their home business conflicts with their family life. By choosing a business that works well for your own family, I believe you can successfully make this work.

It is essential to seek the Lord's will for any home business you are considering. Whether it is done as a family or is primarily your own, it must fit the needs of your family and the plan God has for you. I offer as an illustration the experience I had in deciding to write this book.

I usually jump in with both feet when I see something good. For the first time in my life I actually dragged my feet on what is now one of the most rewarding efforts I have ever made. Through some interesting circumstances (only God could have orchestrated these), I had a small foot in the door at my publisher. As exciting as I found this, I also knew that being a wife, mother, home schooler, and homemaker took every ounce of energy I had every day. These roles are by far my highest priority. Over a six-month period I agonized over even presenting a proposal to the publisher. Once I did, I prayed that the editor would reject it. This probably sounds silly to you, but I was very serious. I really believed that the extra work that comes with working out of my home would tax me beyond all my limits.

I share this with you because seeking the Lord's will is what made this entire experience a good thing for me. When I told a friend how I was praying for the editor to reject my proposal, she told me I should not pray that way. I decided she was right, and I modified my prayer: "Lord, You know that a first-time author who submits one book proposal to one publisher rarely, if ever, gets a positive response. If in my case Crossway Books wants to publish my book, I will take this as a sign from You that it is Your will for me and for my family, and I will gladly write this book for You." After praying this way I felt content because I didn't think Crossway would be interested in the book, and I could not in my own understanding see how I could fit it into my already overflowing schedule.

An interesting thing happened two weeks later. The editor called and said they were interested. The rest is history, but I want you to know that even though I have had a challenging time writing due to a difficult first trimester of a pregnancy and other assorted obstacles, our family has benefited from this endeavor. My husband and I have clarified issues through the writing of this book, and my oldest daughters have perfected their skills in the kitchen beyond my greatest hope. We have learned together as a family and are considering putting together a seminar on this material. All of this came about because it was done in the Lord's will, not my own. As I describe considerations and questions to ask before undertaking a home business, keep in mind the needs of your family and what the Lord would have you do at this particular time in your life.

The first question to ask yourself is, "Why do I want to work at home?" I have already indicated this is not the bed of roses that many people would have you believe. For example, many feel that by working at home you can be home with your children. This is true, but can you work with your children at home? I cannot write with my children hovering around me. I write on days when my husband is home and can take responsibility for the children while I write. This is ideal because they are building their relationship with Dad, and nothing is lost during the time Mom is busy writing. This actually helps us have a more balanced approach in our parenting. We are able to benefit from this arrangement because of our decision to keep Dad home more and live on less.

Some women like to work at home so they can be their own boss. I'm not sure this is true for many businesses because there are so many outside factors that dictate what you are able to do. Do you have to pay a sitter to watch your children? Does the market for your product or service dictate the hours you must work? Is your work seasonal? These are but a few considerations that will affect how much of your own boss you can be. You may not have a person over you telling you what to do, but I find that inconvenient circumstances can be more aggravating than having a boss.

Some women are attracted by the income potential of a home business. The key word here is *potential*. Often the hourly wage for women working out of their home is not high. Particularly during the time you are establishing your business, the hours are long and the pay is low. I would suggest that there be some outside income to support the family during the start-up phase of a business. Husbands should not quit their full-time work until the family business is profitable enough to support the family.

There are good aspects of working out of the home. I did not anticipate working as I am now as an author. We had planned to start a home business sometime in the next couple of years but had not yet developed the idea. What has become a great advantage to me is that during the time I spend writing, I am recharging my batteries. I needed a little outlet for my creative energies that was different from my daily responsibilities. By keeping this in balance with the rest of my life, I have found writing to be an encouragement to me. This is due in part because I am working in an area of my giftedness.

This is a very important point. When you work in an area in which you have a natural inclination or talent, the work is easier. If you select a business that is not tailored to your strengths, you will have to work harder and probably overcome some weaknesses on your part if the business is to succeed. I think it only makes sense to develop your business around your talents. I have a friend who is fluent in Spanish. She has a monthly job with a food company where she translates material for them. She has a certain number of hours per month that she can count on. This work is easy for her and gives her a little break from her daily duties of home schooling her two children. The hourly wage in her case is a good one.

In assessing your talents, think about the things you already do. There may be a market for something you can provide for your family or friends. We are beginning our fourth year of bee-keeping. Jim likes to keep bees, and it gives us all the honey we need. This year we have found a simple arrangement to market our honey and have decided to sell some of it. Gift baskets that you make for your friends could become a home business for you. People may ask you where you got the basket, and when you tell them you made it, they may want you to make one for them for some future occasion. This can be a very casual beginning for a business.

It is my belief that successful home businesses start small. By testing the market you can often see whether or not your ideas will be profitable. By profitable I don't mean just income generating. I think it would be a good idea to forget about the money in the beginning. If you follow what you believe to be God's will for you, He can choose to bless you financially. If you treat your home business as supplemental income, your focus can be on developing your product or service and marketing it well. Word-of-mouth advertising can be a great aid to developing your business. Over time you may find that you have so much business that you are generating a pretty good income.

It is a good idea to set goals for the profits from your business. I sell some phonics curriculum that is very good but not readily available to the home-school community at this time. My purpose in selling this is twofold. I want to share something I really think is a superior product at a very affordable price. I also want to make a little extra money to stretch our curriculum budget. There are always more books I want to purchase.

A business that can train your children in skills they need is a good fit for a family business. My seven- and nine-year-old daughters have given some thought to making and selling whole wheat bread in our neighborhood. Your imagination is really the only limit to what you can develop for your own family.

Does working at home have to generate income? No! Home educating our children is the most challenging and demanding work I have ever undertaken. The rewards are endless, but none of them are in the form of a monthly paycheck. The payback is in the children, who are worth far more than money.

The once-a-month teaching nights (MUG—monthly uplifting get-togethers) are free of charge. I bring women into my home to teach them the concepts from this book. This is also an opportunity for me to show hospitality. It is a very uplifting evening for busy moms. Everyone brings a mug for their drink, and we have a sharing time at the end. Although we have recently set up a resource table, profit is not the motive for this work in my home.

Many blessings come from a business run out of your home. Be aware of the concerns and considerations of such an endeavor, and seek the Lord's will for your family. "Be very careful, then, how you live—not as unwise but as wise, making the most of every opportunity, because the days are evil. Therefore do not be foolish, but understand what the Lord's will is" (Ephesians 5:15-17). Here are a few other verses to help you as you consider a home business:

> *May the God of peace, who through the blood of the eternal covenant brought back from the dead our Lord Jesus, that great Shepherd of the sheep, equip you with everything good for doing his will, and may he work in us what is pleasing to him, through Jesus Christ, to whom be the glory for ever and ever. Amen.*

> —HEBREWS 13:20-21

> *This is the assurance we have in approaching God: that if we ask anything according to his will, he hears us. And if we know that he hears us—whatever we ask—we know that we have what we asked of him.*

> —1 JOHN 5:14-15

Teach me to do your will, for you are my God; may your good Spirit lead me on level ground.

—PSALM 143:10

Whatever you do, work at it with all your heart, as working for the Lord, not for men, since you know that you will receive an inheritance from the Lord as a reward. It is the Lord Christ you are serving.

—COLOSSIANS 3:23-24

10

Home Schooling

THE CHOICE OF WHAT EDUCATIONAL METHOD TO USE FOR YOUR children is a very important one. In a time when public education is under much criticism and private school options are expensive, parents are looking for other alternatives. Whatever you decide, make the decision as an informed parent. I can help you understand a little about the choice being made by many parents—home schooling.

The option of educating children at home is being exercised by more and more parents each year. The number of home-schooling families has begun to grow exponentially. Families have many different reasons for choosing home schooling for their children. Many good books have been written to help you succeed at such an important task. All of this can seem overwhelming if you are just beginning to consider home schooling your children. It will be more manageable if you first examine the issues to consider in making such a decision.

The Bible remains our guidebook for decisions regarding the education of our children, and it gives us direction as to how we are to proceed. We first need to establish when education occurs.

Education is not something that takes place within school hours and ceases at the final bell each day. *Education takes place all the time!* Who, then, should be teaching and training your children?

In Deuteronomy 6:5-7 we read, "Love the LORD your God with all your heart and with all your soul and with all your strength. These commandments that I give you today are to be upon your hearts. Impress them on your children. Talk about them when you sit at home and when you walk along the road, when you lie down and when you get up." Clearly parents are responsible for the spiritual training of their children. The opportunities I have each day to impart spiritual truths to my sons and daughters are endless. If they are not with me, these opportunities are lost. I also create learning opportunities to teach lessons concerning particular areas of weakness for our family. Right now we need to embark on a study of obedience. If my children were off at school, public or private, in different classrooms, they could not benefit from a cohesive family study.

Sure, it's possible to teach this after school hours, but in my view that is improbable. Work schedules, afterschool activities, homework, and sheer exhaustion have made family life all but impossible in our culture. This is not so with home schooling. In that situation we have substantial time to nurture the family unit. This is enhanced by decreasing our income needs and bringing Dad home more.

In our home we train our children. There is a difference between teaching and training. Consider the definition of each as taken from the dictionary. *Teach*: "to impart knowledge of or skill in; give instruction in."[1] *Train*: "to develop or form the habits, thoughts, or behavior of [a child or other person] by discipline and instruction."[2] Schools are in the business of teaching. Knowledge in itself is not bad, but if all your children are being taught is knowledge, they will suffer the consequences. Psalm 119:66 says, " Teach me knowledge and good judgment, for I believe in your commands." The dictionary defines *wisdom* as "knowledge of what is true or right coupled with good judgment."[3]

It is doubtful that our children will learn wisdom in schools if the knowledge that is being taught is not true. It is also impossible for the schools to teach good judgment to a Christian child when Christian principles are not allowed in the school. When public schools are offering politically correct information (horrifying to Christian parents) and Christian schools are using secular textbooks (our local Christian elementary school was using a secular, pro-evolution science text), it is difficult to imagine just what children are being taught in these schools. Training cannot be separated from the Bible, which admonishes us to "Train a child in the way he should go, and when he is old he will not turn from it" (Proverbs 22:6).

The definition of training given above included "instruction" and "discipline." Schools today are not disciplining students effectively. Attempts such as keeping children after school are no longer possible since many students have to go to a day-care situation after school. Corporal punishment was outlawed long ago. How do the schools discipline then? Good question.

I prefer to follow the biblical mandate given in Proverbs 13:24—"He who spares the rod hates his son, but he who loves him is careful to discipline him." Discipline takes many forms, depending on the infraction and the age of the child. Just last night my two oldest daughters (second and fourth grade) received discipline for not copying their misspelled spelling words for two weeks in a row. Usually when they copy the misspelled words as I have instructed, they learn them for the following week without any problem. Since they had failed to complete this assignment for two weeks, they had not learned their words. I required each of them to copy each word missed on yesterday's test fifty times. They found the exercise distasteful, and I doubt they will skip the assignment again. In contrast, public schools are teaching "invented spelling," which means the child doesn't really have to learn to spell.

Beyond academics, morality, values, respect for authority, and biblical training, there exists the issue of peers. Questions are frequently asked about socialization and the home-schooled child. Again we return to the dictionary for a definition. *Socialize*: "make fit for life in companionship with others."[4] It will not be from other children that our kids learn how to behave. Adults must teach children how to behave properly. Putting same-aged children into a room and expecting them to become socialized is foolish at best. It is not a bad thing for children to spend time with their peers, but how it is done makes all the difference. Proverbs 22:15 says, "Folly is bound up in the heart of a child, but the rod of discipline will drive it far from him." Proverbs 13:20 adds, "He who walks with the wise grows wise, but a companion of fools suffers harm." These two verses reinforce for me the notion that children must be supervised. This goes counter to our culture. In the classroom there are many students and only one teacher. Much goes on in a classroom that is unnoticed by the teacher. This lack of supervision contributes to some frightening experiences.

My friend decided to enroll her child in kindergarten after much consideration of home schooling. In less than two weeks her daughter came home with vulgar talk and other inappropriate behaviors she had learned at school. I appreciate the lack of peer pressure that exists in our home school. My children are loved for who they are and are not striving to please another child by engaging in something we do not endorse. Once children enter school, they are exposed to all the other values the school teaches as well as to the lives of other children. In a culture where divorce, abortion, and homosexuality are deemed normal, I prefer to know about the families of the boys and girls who will be spending time with my children.

If you have never considered home schooling, these thoughts may sound a bit radical to you. I don't apologize for that. We live in a time in history when we need to take some radical steps. The schools are very different than what we experienced as children. I remember a time when we were in trouble if we chewed gum. Principals and teachers are now having to be concerned with guns being brought to school. Two-parent families used to raise children. Now many children bounce between divorced parents or have been raised primarily in day care since birth. Politically correct information that is being taught is inappropriate for our children. Even if you live in an area that has good schools, be aware of just how much influence an increasingly godless federal government has on those schools.

As a Christian parent, you need to understand what is being taught in the school your child attends. You must ask questions. Are teachers, in the name of multiculturalism, teaching respect for cultural differences, or are your children being taught to accept the worship of other gods or unbiblical worldviews? It is possible that your children are being taught that it is right and good to tolerate sin. What is the impact of our nation's preferential treatment of homosexuals? What does public-school curriculum say? Books such as *Heather Has Two Mommies* have already been read in the public schools.

These thoughts are intended to help you evaluate your own decision as to how to educate your children. Our family has chosen to home school. You may choose another alternative. Whatever you decide, do so as an informed parent. Find out what really goes on in the classroom. Talk to other parents who have had difficulties with the school and decided to home school. Children are too precious to trust to an institution that may not be worthy of your trust.

11

A Final
Word

WHEW! THAT WAS A LOT OF MATERIAL. I MYSELF AM CHALLENGED as I see the comprehensive nature of this book and realize how many areas there are in our lives where we need to be competent. You will recall that I did not begin my journey as a homemaker knowing what I have shared with you. It is over many years, through much trial and error, that I have learned to run my home somewhat efficiently.

I cannot stress enough the importance of remembering that this work covers so many areas of life that you cannot possibly hope to attack it all at once. I don't believe we can rely on our own thinking to decide where to begin. Involve your family in the process of change. Find out what matters most to each one of them. Likely there will be varying answers. You will need to consult yet another source as well—make sure you talk to God about all this. Don't forget this absolutely crucial step!

God's role in helping you absorb what is most important for your own family is a vital one. In my old patterns of thinking, I used to size up a situation and then make decisions. I know now that this leaves out God's plan for me and my family. God has a special plan for each one of us, and usually all of the details are not revealed right away. If I base my decisions on only what I can see and understand, I will fail to see the bigger picture that God has planned for me. Even though I know all of this, I find it difficult to stop trying to do everything in my own power. Some Bible verses help me remember that I am not in this alone.

In his letter to the Philippians Paul writes about the life of a Christian: "being confident of this, that he who began a good work in you will carry it on to completion until the day of Christ Jesus" (1:6). If you are feeling that the workload you are carrying is more than you can possibly handle, remember that God doesn't expect you to do it alone. He doesn't expect us to learn all we need to know about running our homes all at once. This verse talks about the learning process and His provision and help, continuing until Christ returns. Pace yourself; rely on God's daily presence as part of the plan.

Another passage conveys my life verses—Philippians 1:9-10: "And this is my prayer: that your love may abound more and more in knowledge and depth of insight, so that you may be able to discern what is best and may be pure and blameless until the day of Christ." It has been refreshing to learn that I don't need to strive to get everything done. I simply need to be able, with the Lord's help, on a daily basis, to decide what is best for that day and do it! As I did research for this book, I found a lot of information that I want to put into practice in my own home. I am in the same place you are right now. I have to decide what is best to spend my time on at this point in my life.

I need to be constantly aware that I tend to feel I have to accomplish everything by working hard at it myself. While hard work is important, it is not the only way the job gets done. Hebrews 13:20-21 says, "May the God of peace, who through the blood of the eternal covenant brought back from the dead our Lord Jesus, that great Shepherd of the sheep, equip you with everything good for doing his will, and may he work in us what is pleasing to him, through Jesus Christ, to whom be glory for ever and ever. Amen." This is a powerful verse in terms of our roles as wives, mothers, teachers, employees, and whatever else we do. My book is hopefully a tool you can use, but it is God who will equip you for whatever He is calling you to do.

I know what you may be thinking because I think it too: How is God going to do all this? I like to know the game plan ahead of time (you know how I love structure). Most importantly, I want to know where my energy will be coming from. As I wrote this chapter I was seven months pregnant during the hot summer months. I didn't feel very energetic. Truthfully, I wanted to sit down for the next two months, sip iced tea, and wait for the baby to be born. But life doesn't work that way. Fortunately, the Bible promises that the energy we need will be there when we need it. In Psalm 18 David reflects on the strength of his enemies and how they were too strong for him. In verse 32 we read: "It is God who arms me with strength and makes my way perfect." David felt overwhelmed, just as we do at times; but he acknowledged the source of his strength as God, not himself.

Similarly, other verses remind us that God can work mightily during our times of weakness. Romans 8:26 says, "The Spirit helps us in our weakness. We do not know what we ought to pray, but the Spirit himself intercedes for us with groans that words cannot express." Have you ever had one of those days where you just could not get anything to come together? It can be so overwhelming. You don't have a clue how to solve your problems or even what to pray for in such a case. Take heart—the Holy Spirit is always there for us during our times of weakness.

In 2 Corinthians 12 Paul talks about a problem he had that he referred to as "a thorn in my flesh." He asked the Lord to take away his weakness three times, but the Lord responded, "My grace is sufficient for you, for my power is made perfect in weakness" (v. 9). I assume that each of you is feeling weak in some area that I have covered or you would not have picked up this book.

Even though I pretty much know what to do, I feel weak in some of these areas at times too. I would no doubt find myself consumed with discouragement if it were not for my relationship with the Lord Jesus Christ.

For a long time I did not know what it meant to have a relationship with Jesus. I attended church fairly regularly as a teenager and then again after I was married. Jim and I heard many sermons without ever really understanding the role Jesus could play in our lives if we chose to let Him do so. We were married for five years before we finally understood. I can offer you techniques and shortcuts, but that won't truly make you happy. Only by first building the right foundation through a personal relationship with Jesus Christ can what I have shared with you become possible. "Unless the LORD builds the house, its builders labor in vain" (Psalm 127:1). I don't want to finish this book without making sure I have shared the Scriptures that led me to know Jesus as my Savior, so you can be sure you know Him too! Perhaps you already do, but if not, I urge you to seriously consider what I am about to share.

How can we go to heaven when our time on earth is over? "Jesus answered, 'I am the way and the truth and the life. No one comes to the Father except through me" (John 14:6). Because we are all born with a sin nature, we are separated from God. "For all have sinned and fall short of the glory of God" (Romans 3:23). "For the wages of sin is death, but the gift of God is eternal life in Christ Jesus our Lord" (Romans 6:23). The death of Christ on the cross took the punishment for our sins. "For what I received I passed on to you as of first importance: that Christ died for our sins according to the Scriptures, that he was buried, that he was raised on the third day according to the Scriptures" (1 Corinthians 15:3-4).

Our relationship with Jesus begins as we believe these truths and ask Him through prayer to become our Lord and Savior. "For God so loved the world that he gave his one and only Son, that whoever believes in him shall not perish but have eternal life" (John 3:16). "Yet to all who received him, to those who believed in his name, he gave the right to become children of God" (John 1:12). "For it is by grace you have been saved, through faith—and this not from yourselves, it is the gift of God—not by works, so that no one can boast" (Ephesians 2:8-9).

Now that we have established a firm foundation, let's examine what the home of an author on homemaking skills really looks like—a "reality check." What has my life been like during the writing of this book? Have the principles I have shared worked out in my family? First, I had to lower my standards in some areas, food being the area that suffered the most. Usually there are times during a pregnancy when we end up eating out more often, but while I wrote this book we have eaten out too much! (Those of you who live in the country, consider yourself blessed if you have few restaurants. We have one on every corner, which doesn't exactly force me to make sure we eat at home.) I have really been feeling guilty about this eating out business since it usually costs us between $25 and $30 per meal. It came to me one night that if we have saved a couple of thousand dollars by using cloth diapers, we could spring for a few meals at a restaurant. Don't feel guilty if you finally improve upon an area and then slump back into old patterns due to special circumstances. The key to success is to get back on track and do things the right way as soon as you can.

Another area that I have totally blown during the writing of this book is exercise. My half-hour daily walks were a well-established pattern that just fell apart in the last few months. And there is still the issue of my desk! Jim does not understand why I refer to him as a "messie" in my book when my desk is such a wreck. I guess he has a point.

You may be interested to know some of the incidents that took place in our home while I was writing this book. My three-year-old, Jonathan, decided to try to give himself a haircut.

Fortunately, we stopped him before much damage was done. My new flannel sheets (white) came out of the dryer with grease on them. A red rug was washed with some white items that are now pink. I had my own laundry disaster that included a couple of crayons making it all the way through the dryer (the crayons no longer existed when I took the load out; they were a series of permanent color blotches that hit nearly every article of clothing in that white load). The baby was found chewing on the end of the plunger for the toilet. Yuck! While Jamie was cooking, one of our kitchen towels caught fire. As I was writing the chapter on food, we had a small fire on top of our stove. Jim was home during the time I was writing, so these things occurred as part of the normal flow of life at our house.

As you can see, maintaining balance is a constant struggle. I can't keep everything running at peak performance all at the same time. As soon as I work to become strong in one area, I notice that another area is weak. Remember that you are filling many roles all at once. Forget perfection! Rather, strive for competency in all areas. While we are aiming for balance, we must be armed with the knowledge that we will be somewhat out of balance most of the time.

Don't be alarmed if even though you know what to do, you can't seem to make it work. Paul had a similar struggle, which he shared in Romans 7:15-25. His struggle was with his sin nature (the old Paul—who he was before coming to Jesus Christ as his Savior), but one verse stands out to me regarding my own inability to apply what I know at times: "I do not understand what I do. For what I want to do I do not do, but what I hate I do" (v. 15). Our struggle is with the sin nature too. Satan does not want families to be strong. Any steps you make to strengthen your family are not welcomed by the enemy of our souls. This may be why we find it difficult to do what we know we should. Prayer is a major part of the answer to this problem.

I would like to share my own personal plan for change with

you. I am very much in process, just as you are, and I always need to be mindful of what areas I should be working on. My plans right now are not big ones as I wrap up a year and a half of working on this book just weeks before the birth of my sixth child. I realize that I need to reflect on the many things I have learned in recent months. I won't be reading much for a while, so I can process what I have already read. I need to rest physically both before the birth and afterwards. The one project that has been nagging me is my cookbook and how it needs to be reorganized. Jim helped me these last few weeks by making our bread and had trouble because some of the changes I make in the recipe I just have in my head. I want to make my cookbook more family-friendly, so anyone can use it successfully. This type of work is mental work with minimum physical effort. It will lay the foundation for our winter project of expanding our food horizons once again. (I am sick of eating out!) If time permits, I would like to make a few new nursing dresses too.

When I set up a plan such as the one above, I have learned to be careful about how I evaluate my progress. I am going to focus on how I am improving, not how close I am to the final goal. If circumstances prevent me from fixing up my cookbook exactly the way I want it, I will be encouraged by the fact that it is more useful than it was when I started. You can make yourself crazy by keeping your eyes on the completed goal and neglecting to notice how much progress you are making. I don't know what you need to work on first, but here are some ideas for a simple plan to get you going.

- Begin baking your own bread.
- Reduce your food budget.
- Decide to buy five food items in bulk, and set up a food storage system.
- Clean one room (possibly the living room), keep it clutter-free. Go to this room to work on plans for other changes.

- Make half of this year's Christmas gifts.
- Turn down your thermostat or turn off your air conditioning.
- Set up a new service (chore) system for your children.
- Commit thirty minutes per day to reading your Bible.

Remember the wood-burning stove? Well, I got through the first winter. Unfortunately, I only had a "get through the winter" attitude about it. There are many benefits of heating with wood, but the drawbacks seemed to affect me the most. I complained when it was too chilly, and I grumbled about having to put another log in when my husband was working. Our attitudes really make or break the changes we are trying to make. Much of the time our attitudes deteriorate because we are tired or frustrated. Keep the following Scripture verses on a notecard, and pull them out when you need encouragement. Remember, you don't have to do it all by yourself. Someone is at hand to help you.

Even youths grow tired and weary, and young men stumble and fall; but those who hope in the Lord will renew their strength. They will soar on wings like eagles; they will run and not grow weary, they will walk and not be faint.

—ISAIAH 40:30-31

Let me know how the changes are coming at your household. Tell me what has helped you the most. May God be with you!

EQUIPPING THE FAMILY
ATTN: JACKIE
P.O. BOX 3202
GLEN ELLYN, IL 60138-3202

Appendix A:
—
Daily Flow Chart

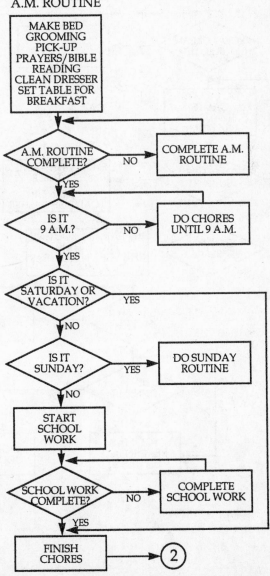

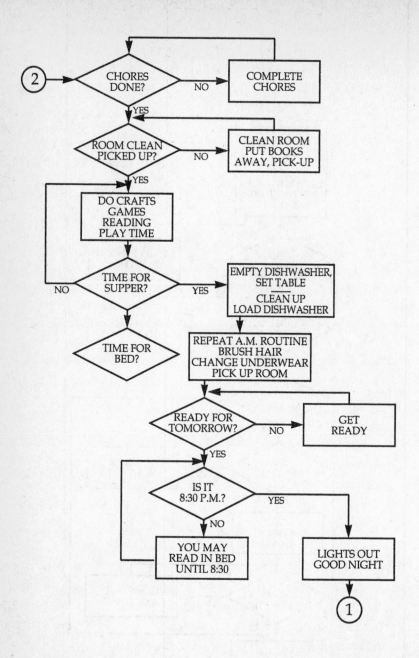

Appendix B:

—

Miscellaneous Resources for the Homemaker

MOPs International (Mothers of Preschoolers)
1311 S. Clarkson Street
Denver, CO 80210
303-733-5353

Call them to find the nearest MOPs group in your area.

The Christian Mom's Ideas Book by Ellen Banks Elwell, Crossway Books, Wheaton, IL, 1997. This compilation of thoughts from eighty-two moms gives over 500 useful tips. The ideas are arranged categorically, covering just a few pages for each topic. Perfect for busy moms with only a minute or two to glean some practical encouragement. I love this one!

MAGAZINES

Crowned with Silver—Godly Homemaking Wisdom from Bygone Eras, P.O. Box 144, Florence, CO 81226-0144. This is a unique publication that includes pieces written by godly women who lived more than 100 years ago. Guidance is given in areas such as courtship, marriage, hospitality, manners, child training, and home remedies. I very much appreciate the wisdom from the older ladies being passed along to those of us who are younger.

Welcome Home, Mothers at Home, 8310A Old Courthouse Road, Vienna, VA 22182. This magazine is for the woman who has chosen to make the nurture of her family a top priority. For a mother with young children or a mother who has just left the workforce, *Welcome Home* is a friend during what could be a lonely time. Through its pages you will read of the joys and frustrations of countless others who are also staying home to raise their families. Articles are short and easy to read in the five-minute blocks of time that mothers have to read.

An Encouraging Word, P.O. Box 599, Idabel, OK 74745. This may very well be my favorite magazine. It is loaded with useful information on homemaking issues, as well as encouragement in areas that can be a struggle to all of us. I especially benefit from reading the personal stories of women who worked through their disappointments, impatience, discontent, and other commonly experienced emotions. Other bonuses include information on current government proposals that affect the family, advice from a midwife, and so much more!

The Family Messenger, P.O. Box 130, Woodbury, TN 37190. This is a magazine for the entire family. The publishers' purpose is to "build up, establish and if necessary, repair and reconstruct the home." Biblical teaching by the male head of the family is viewed as strong and sound. They encourage home-owned and/or operated businesses by describing different options in detail. Recipes, child training, and powerful articles by guest authors are included. This is a magazine truly devoted to equipping the Christian family.

The Homemaker's Forum, The Urban Homemaker, P.O. Box 440967, Aurora, CO 80044; phone: 800-55-BREAD. If you are serious about learning how to cook more economical and nutritious foods, this is for you. In addition to the excellent recipes from readers, there are so many quick tips that you are sure to be inspired.

Above Rubies, P.O. Box 351, Antioch, TN 37011-0351. This magazine is published to encourage women in their roles as wives, mothers, and homemakers. The editor states, "Its purpose is to uphold and strengthen family life and to raise the standard of God's truth in the nation." It is the publisher's desire to publish quarterly, but realistically the magazine comes out a couple of times per year. It is a non-subscription magazine supported solely by contributions. As funds are available, the magazine is printed. Begun twenty years ago in New Zealand, this publication includes articles and letters from all over the world, making it truly unique. I love it!

—

Further
Resources

ONE OF MY GOALS IN WRITING THIS BOOK WAS TO PROVIDE women with one book that would cover numerous important topics so it would not be necessary to read many books just to get started in these different areas.

The reason I have reviewed so many resources for you in this section is that I know some of you will want to know where to look for more in-depth information. In many cases there will be one book that can do the job, but I have reviewed three or four that will work. By no means do I intend for you to go out and buy everything I suggest.

Many titles can be found in public libraries or church libraries. Magazine subscriptions can be shared with a friend. In no way have I exhausted the resources I recommend, nor will I use all of them myself. Just as I have been stressing the uniqueness of your family, you too are unique. A book that you absolutely love may not suit the needs of your friend.

Doctrinal differences exist, and by no means am I endorsing every word found in every resource I recommend. The only perfect book is the Bible, so be aware that all other books contain flaws. I would encourage you to take any questions back to Scripture (possibly with the guidance of your pastor) and settle the matter there. Each of us needs to examine resources in light of what we find useful and correct, and forget the rest. With this mind-set you can still use a book that may contain a few things you disagree with and benefit from the experience.

This is why I have included so many choices. Be sure to examine them for yourself to be certain they are suitable for you

Resources—
Chapter 1: Lifestyle Simplification

BOOKS

Little House on The Freeway by Tim Kimmel, Sisters, OR: Multnomah, 1994. The author builds his perception of a simplified lifestyle around the topic of rest. Through anecdotes and suggestions for personal application, the concept of rest is developed as it applies to marriage, children, work, and relationships. Most encouraging!

'Tis a Gift to be Simple—Embracing the Freedom of Living with Less, by Barbara DeGrote-Sorensen and David Allen Sorensen, Minneapolis: Augsburg Fortress, 1992. This is a good resource if you desire greater understanding of why you should simplify your life. Their list of ten reasons for choosing a simpler lifestyle is a springboard for further discussion of biblical principles applicable to the process.

Six Weeks to a Simpler Lifestyle by Barbara DeGrote-Sorensen and David Allen Sorensen, Minneapolis: Augsburg Fortress, 1994. Based on the concept that it takes six weeks to develop a habit, this follow-up book to the one above gives you practical suggestions for making changes. This book can be used as a Bible study and contains ideas for using it in a small group.

A Place Called Simplicity—The Quiet Beauty of Simple Living by

Claire Cloninger, Eugene, OR: Harvest House, 1993. This refreshing book chronicles the author's journey from city living to her quiet cabin in the country. She defines simplicity as a person— Jesus. Her personal stories combined with her biblical insights into simplicity make this one of my favorites on this topic.

Downscaling—Simplify and Enrich Your Lifestyle by Dave and Kathy Babbitt, Chicago: Moody Press, 1993. Corporate downsizing in the business world solves certain problems, and downscaling in our lifestyles can be the answer to many problems in our family life. The authors' personal anecdotes and the testimonies of others will be particularly encouraging to the woman moving out of a fast-track career.

The Encyclopedia of Country Living, 9th edition by Carla Emery, Seattle: Sasquatch Books, 1994. This book is written for everyone—from the city dweller with a little room for a garden to the homesteader living off the land. It is very interesting reading, yet intensely practical. Over 800 pages long, it is filled with resources, illustrations, and a style of writing that is sure to make you smile.

Margin, Restoring Emotional, Physical, Financial, and Time Reserves to Overloaded Lives by Richard A. Swenson, M.D., Colorado Springs: NavPress, 1992. In an era of too many choices, too much to do, overwhelming demands, and the like, this book is a welcome refreshment to our overworked culture. "Margin" is defined as "having breath left at the top of the staircase, money left at the end of the month, and sanity left at the end of adolescence." Prescriptions for good living include contentment, simplicity, balance, and rest.

Running on Empty and Looking for the Nearest Exit by Annie Chapman, Minneapolis: Bethany House, 1995. Anyone who feels they are on the verge of collapse will appreciate the author's humorous approach to dealing with this problem. This balanced perspective is enhanced by the author's transparent sharing of her own struggles. Many songs that Steve and Annie Chapman have written are included here, further making this an inspiring book.

Living More with Less by Doris Janzen Longacre, Scottdale, PA: Herald Press, 1980. Written from a perspective influenced by the worldwide experiences of Mennonites, this book offers specific how-to information while inspiring the reader with thought-provoking testimonies. This is the most serious book on simplifying your life that I have found.

MAGAZINES

Coming Home, P.O. Box 367, Savannah, TN 38372. Articles and resources in this publication are centered around concerns of the home in the context of simple living. The practical advice makes this a good choice for those who have moved to the country or for folks like us who want to but haven't gotten there yet. This definitely has a homesteader's flavor.

Countryside and Small Stock Journal, W11564 Highway 64, Withee, WI, 54498; phone: 800-551-5691. This is a simple living journal filled with practical encouragement for homesteaders. It is targeted toward those who prefer country life and desire to be less dependent on others to supply their needs. Articles such as the one about a log cabin built for $12,000 by a family with a $2,400 annual income are inspiring.

American Small Farm, Magnet Communications, Inc., 21822 Sherman Way, Suite 200, Canoga Park, CA 91303; phone: 818-716-3131. Although designed for people on small farms and ranches, we have found articles about growing plants in a greenhouse and dwarf fruit trees to be useful to us in the suburbs. This magazine is very helpful if you are planning to move to a rural location. They offer a source book that can help you locate just about anything.

CATALOGS

Peaceful Valley Farm Supply, P.O. Box 2209, Grass Valley, CA 95945; phone: 916-272-4769. Committed to sustainable agriculture, this catalog has over 100 pages of tools and supplies for organic farming and gardening.

Cumberland General Store, Route 3, Crossville, TN 38555; phone: 800-334-4640. Nearly 300 pages of old-time general merchandise with many simple living items for life on the homestead.

Lehman's Non-Electric Catalog, 4779 Kidron Road, P.O. Box 41, Kidron, OH 44636; phone: 216-857-5757. For those who live without electricity, this is a must-have catalog. We found much information that helped us when we purchased our oil lamps and our wood stove.

Resources—
Chapter 2: Healthy Living

BOOKS

Health Begins in Him—Biblical Steps to Optimal Health and Nutrition by Terry Dorian, Lafayette, LA: Huntington House, 1995. Having cured her own health problems through a whole-foods dietary regime, the author clearly and specifically tells us how to do the same. Biblical principles are applied to health and nutrition in an easy-to-understand format.

The Cookbook, Health Begins in Him by Terry Dorian, Lafayette, LA: Vital Issues Press, 1997. This collection of over 100 healthy recipes will help you implement the Phase One and Phase Two regimens for optimal health presented in the author's first book. The recipes by Rita Thomas demonstrate that healthy whole foods really can taste good!

Green Pastures—The New Resource Guide, Vital Food Sources, Inc., P.O. Box 1367, Flat Rock, NC 28731; phone: 800-295-3477. Terry Dorian carries an interesting selection of products to help you in your quest for health. These products are tested to assure you of their potency. Call for a catalog!

Eating Better Program Guide by Terry Dorian, Salt Lake City: Nutriflex, 1993; phone: 800-888-8587. This book is full of basic information on eating well that many of us never learned.

Vitamins, minerals, herbs, freshly milled flour, food dehydration, food intolerance, and recipes are presented so clearly that I am including this book as required reading for our daughters in preparation for feeding their own families.

Healthy Habits—20 Simple Ways to Improve Your Health by David and Anne Frahm, Colorado Springs: Piñon Press, 1993. Having cured her own terminal cancer through changes in diet and nutrition, Anne shares her vast knowledge in this book. Not only telling you what to do, but also why you should do it, the authors expand on many of the issues I raised in this chapter.

David and Anne Frahm also run Health Quarters Lodge, P.O. Box 62130, Colorado Springs, 80962; phone: 719-593-8694. This retreat center is the perfect opportunity to enjoy the beauty of the Rocky Mountains while learning how to make lifestyle changes that will move you toward better health. It will certainly provide a life-changing experience for those committed to improving their health. Be sure to ask about their newsletter, *Health Quarterly*.

Food Smart—Eat Your Way to Better Health by Cheryl Townsley, Colorado Springs: Pinon Press, 1994. The author shares her story of recovery after unsuccessfully trying to commit suicide. At her lowest point, she shares, "My overweight, tired, sick body just didn't care, or have the energy to care, about anything." While the practical tips are wonderful, I am drawn by her testimony of how a fast-track professional career completely destroyed her health. I highly recommend this book to the professional woman who feels that everything is about to close in on her.

Kid Smart! Raising a Healthy Child by Cheryl Townsley, Lifestyle for Health Publishing, P.O. Box 3871, Littleton, CO 80161, 1996; phone: 303-771-9357. The author speaks from her experience of learning to change her attitudes toward food and nutrition. Her focus is on how to work with children as you move them toward health. This book is loaded with practical how-to information as well as kid-friendly recipes.

Prescription for Nutritional Healing, 2nd edition, by James

F. Balch, M.D. and Phyllis A. Balch, C.N.C, Garden City Park, NY: Avery Publishing Group, 1997. Beyond discussing the elements of health and various remedies and therapies, this book lists common medical problems in an easy-to-use alphabetical listing. Suggestions regarding essential nutrients, herbs, vitamin supplements, and minerals and other recommendations make this book useful when dealing with illness. I use this reference often.

Prescription for Cooking and Dietary Wellness, revised edition by Phyllis A. Balch, C.N.C. and James F. Balch, M.D., Greenfield, IN: P.A.B. Publishing, Inc., 1992. This book is much like an encyclopedia on nutrition. Wellness charts indicating which vitamins, minerals, vegetables, nuts, grains, seeds, fruits, and herbs will help specific body parts are very helpful if you are trying to deal with health problems through diet modification. Half of the book is recipes, and the other half has benefits too numerous to mention. This is one of the most useful books I own.

Smart Medicine for a Healthier Child—A Practical A-To-Z Reference to Natural and Conventional Treatments for Infants and Children by Janet Zand, Rachel Walton, R.N., and Bob Rountree, M.D., Garden City Park, NY: Avery Publishing Group, 1994. This is the first book I turn to when one of our children becomes ill. In addition to conventional remedies for various ailments, natural alternatives are presented to give you more options. While I don't agree with all the remedies presented, it sure is nice to be able to choose between several alternatives.

Childhood Ear Infections—What Every Parent and Physician Should Know About Prevention, Home Care, and Alternative Treatment by Michael A. Schmidt, M.D., Berkeley, CA: North Atlantic Books, 1990. This book was a big help to us after our first four children suffered chronic ear infections—three of them ending up with tubes. Determined to find a better way, we read this book and purposed to use alternative treatment with our fifth child. She is almost two years old and has had two ear infections that were diagnosed by a doctor and cleared up by methods that did not include antibiotics. My doctor's response was that he could not argue with our results. Check it out!

Beyond Antibiotics—50 (Or So) Ways to Boost Immunity and Avoid Antibiotics by Michael A. Schmidt, M.D., Lendon H. Smith, M.D., and Keith W. Sehnert, M.D., Berkeley, CA: North Atlantic Books, 1994. This book contains valuable information for anyone committed to building the immune system in their quest for health. Particularly enlightening is the chapter on environmental threats to your immune system. There is much to be learned here that you probably won't be able to find out from your doctor.

Aunt Sally's Tried and True Home Remedies, Avenel, NJ: Gramercy Books, 1993. This book is a compilation of home remedies. The notes were preserved by the author's family, making available to us many old-fashioned remedies for a host of different problems. I found this book to be as entertaining as it was useful.

SPIRITUAL HEALTH

The True Woman by Susan Hunt, Wheaton, IL: Crossway Books, 1997. At a time when the biblical role of women is so poorly understood, this book clarifies the portrait of a godly woman. Scriptural accounts of women coupled with stories shared by women of today illustrate the author's powerful message regarding what it means to be a true woman. A study of this book could do wonders for your spiritual health!

Spiritual Intimacy for Couples by Charles and Virginia Sell, Wheaton, IL: Crossway Books, 1996. Many married couples miss the benefits of spiritual intimacy because they don't know how to make it a vital part of their relationship. Enjoy this resource that includes not only the insights of the authors, but thoughts from attendees of their marriage seminars and those who responded to their questionnaire. Be encouraged that your problems are not unusual; share the joy of successfully overcoming these through the suggestions you will learn from this book. This can either be studied together with your husband or read by yourself to use as a springboard for discussion.

A Woman's Walk with God—A Daily Guide for Prayer and Spiritual Growth by Sheila Cragg, Wheaton, IL: Crossway Books, 1996. Superior as a beginning for those who have never before had a devotional life. Encouraging to all women in pursuing a devotional lifestyle rather than merely a regimented quiet time. In the context of teaching *how* to have a disciplined devotional life, the author includes daily devotionals reinforcing the teaching. This book works well for personal or group study and is highly recommended.

Becoming His Masterpiece by April O. Kinzinger, P.O. Box 1, Carlock, IL 61725. This prayer journal is an excellent tool to begin a regular recording of your prayer life. Sections entitled "My Worship," " My Confession," "My Petitions," "My Gratefulness," "Bible Study," and "Sermon Notes" are complete with instructions and examples. This is quite helpful for someone like me who needed some instruction on *how* to keep a prayer journal effectively.

Homemaking—A Bible Study for Women at Home by Baukje Doornenbal and Tjitske Lemstra, Colorado Springs: NavPress, 1981. This study affirms the woman who chooses to stay at home and be a homemaker. I spent three and a half years working through this study, which laid the foundation for much of what I am doing today. Highly recommended!

A Mother's Legacy—Encouragement from Mothers of the Bible by Jeanne Hendricks, Colorado Springs: NavPress, 1988. When motherhood is about to overwhelm you, rest assured— others have gone before you, and you can learn from their examples. This study covers eleven mothers in the Bible and is designed in a format that can fit into the busiest of schedules.

The Power of Motherhood—What the Bible Says About Mothers by Nancy Campbell, Above Rubies, P.O. Box 351, Antioch, TN 37011-0351, 1996. This study of motherhood written by a godly mother of six grown children gives encouragement to mothers. I am encouraged and refreshed every time I open this book. Highly recommended!

Quiet Reflections for Mothers by Nancy Campbell, Above Rubies, P.O. Box 351, Antioch, TN 37011-0351, 1996. This collection of 101 poems for mothers is just the uplifting kind of material you can read when you only have a minute or two. Loaded with just the right wisdom to calm a busy mom during a difficult day. I turn to this book when I need to regain my perspective.

The Joy of Hospitality by Dee Brestin, Wheaton, IL: Victor Books, 1993. Opening our homes to others is rapidly becoming a lost art in modern America. This study focuses on the joy that comes from hospitality and the biblical principles that define this area of service.

Lord Bless My Child by William and Nancie Carmichael, Wheaton, IL: Tyndale House, 1995. This prayer journal is divided into fifty-two chapters covering one character quality per week. Each chapter begins with a Scripture verse followed by a prayer. Insights and reflections on each character quality make this a unique book. This would make an excellent gift for a family with a new baby.

Proverbs for Busy Women, edited by Mary C. Busha, Nashville: Broadman and Holman, 1995. This three-volume set includes devotions written by various women covering strengthening your walk with God, building up your relationships, and refreshing you in your work. Each devotion begins with a verse of Scripture, ends with a prayer, and is short enough to complete during a short block of time that we can all find in our days. I appreciate the many perspectives shared by the different authors.

EMOTIONAL HEALTH

Motherhood Is Stranger Than Fiction by Mary Chambers, Downers Grove, IL: InterVarsity Press, 1995. A sense of humor is important to a mother's health. This collection of cartoons drawn by a mother of six will surely spark laughter in any mother. Reading through the book reminded me of how funny our common motherhood experiences can be if we just give ourselves permission to laugh.

Resources—
Chapter 3: Food

ONCE A MONTH COOKING

Dinner's in the Freezer by Jill Bond, The Bonding Place, P.O. Box 736, Lake Hamilton, FL 33851. More than a cookbook, this is a system designed to help you provide meals for your family efficiently and economically. The author combines personal anecdotes, philosophy, and recipes to make this a useful tool to help you be a successful once-a-month cook.

Meals in 30 Minutes, 2nd edition by Cheryl Townsley, Lifestyle for Health Publishing, P.O. Box 3871, Littleton, CO 80161, 1995; phone: 303-771-9357. This convenient spiral-bound cookbook contains much more than recipes. Each recipe has a nutritional analysis, and some have ingredient substitution suggestions. A creative cooking section and a preferred brand list complete with addresses are but two of the helpful features in this book.

Cooking What Comes Naturally by Nikki Goldbeck, Ceres Press, Woodstock, NY 1981. This book presents a month of vegetarian menus that will help you design your nutritious meals without using meat. Although it is not geared toward putting meals away in the freezer, many of the recipes are simple to prepare and are made from ingredients commonly found at the grocery store. This would certainly enhance your monthly food plan.

COOKBOOKS

Make-a-Mix by Karine Eliason, Nevada Harward, & Madeline Westover, Fisher Books, 4239 West Ina Road, Suite 101, Tucson,

AZ 85741, 1995. Meals are prepared much more quickly when using premade mixes. This book contains sixty-seven different mixes that make over 300 recipes. This is a great resource for the woman who wants to stop using prepared mixes from the store but doesn't want to sacrifice the convenience.

Lifestyle for Health-Smart Cooking for Busy People, 2nd edition by Cheryl Townsley, Lifestyle for Health Publishing, P.O. Box 3871, Littleton, CO 80161, 1995; phone: 303-771-9357. Here is a good book to teach you how to cook healthier food. Recipes are simple and specific, making this a good book for the beginner and the experienced alike. This is a superior resource for learning how to use new ingredients successfully.

Sue Gregg's Eating Better Cookbooks by Sue Gregg, Eating Better Cookbooks, 8830 Glencoe Drive, Riverside, CA 92503; phone: 800-998-2783. All seven of her cookbooks that I own have been a great help in improving the quality of our diet. *Main Dishes*, *Meals in Minutes*, *Soups and Muffins*, *Lunches and Snacks*, *Breakfasts*, *Desserts*, and *Yeast Breads* contain much how-to information, including why you should do certain things a specific way. The cookbooks are recipes and a cooking class all rolled into one. Contact the publisher for more information regarding their other products.

The 15 Minute Meal Planner—A Realistic Approach to a Healthy Lifestyle by Emilie Barnes and Sue Gregg, Eugene, OR: Harvest House Publishers, 1994. If you are motivated to change your diet but don't know where to begin, here is the place. This comprehensive book is written in fifty-nine quick-to-read chapters explaining just about everything you ever wanted to know about food. Twelve of the chapters fall under the heading "Biblical Perspectives." This book is a good value.

Whole Foods for the Whole Family, edited by Roberta Bishop Johnson, LaLeche League International, P.O. Box 4079, 1400 N. Meacham Road, Schaumburg, IL 60168-4079, 1993; phone: 847-519-7730. This revised edition of a kitchen classic is sure to perk up your healthy meals. These recipes are intended for use by families who want to eat minimally processed whole foods.

American Wholefoods Cuisine by Nikki and David Goldbeck, New York: NAL Books, 1983. This is the first "healthy" cookbook that I owned. Over the past thirteen years our family has been introduced to exciting new tastes through the wholesome recipes found here. Some say this book replaces *The Joy of Cooking* for those seeking a healthy diet.

More with Less Cookbook by Doris Janzen Longacre, Scottdale, PA: Herald Press, 1976. This is a cookbook for the woman who wants to use simple, basic ingredients to feed her family nutritious food at a minimum cost. I especially like the section on soybeans. This book is written in a style that will be attractive to those wishing to simplify their lifestyles.

Country Ground Beef, Reiman Publications; order from Country Store, Offer 3318, 5925 Country Lane, P.O. Box 990, Greendale, WI 53129, 1993; phone: 800-558-1013. This cookbook offers nearly 300 recipes that are sure to please the pickiest of carnivores. You can substitute ground turkey and use less than the amount called for in a recipe if you want to lower the fat content. There are many pictures of the recipes showing how to serve them.

Country Beans by Rita Bingham, Natural Meals in Minutes, 30500 SE Jackson Rd., Gresham, OR 97080, 1996; phone: 800-484-9377, ext. 6276. More than just a collection of bean recipes, this book uses bean flours in a variety of ways. Wheat-free and gluten-free recipes make this especially useful for those with allergies. This is healthy eating!

DESSERTS

Smart Cookies by Jane Kinderlehrer, New York: Newmarket Press, 1985. This is the healthiest collection of cookie recipes I have ever seen. Check your library or used bookstores for this one.

Sweet and Natural-Desserts Without Sugar, Honey,

Molasses or Artificial Sweeteners by Janet Warrington, Freedom, CA: The Crossing Press, 1991. This creatively organized collection of very healthy recipes proves that there is such a thing as a healthy dessert.

HARVEST/CANNING

Bountiful Harvest, Reiman Publications; order from Country Store, Offer 3318, 5925 Country Lane, P.O. Box 990, Greendale, WI 53129, 1994; phone: 800-558-1013. At last there is a book to help you use up your garden harvest in so many taste-tempting ways. Beautiful pictures make the recipes come to life. This will surely encourage you in your gardening efforts.

Putting It Up with Honey—A Natural Foods Canning and Preserving Cookbook by Susan Geiskopf, Quicksilver Productions, P.O. Box 340, Ashland, OR 97520, 1984. Our first attempt using this cookbook yielded fabulous canned peaches. There are many recipes for jelly, jam, and preserves.

The Busy Person's Guide to Preserving Food by Janet Chadwick, Storey Communications, Inc., Schoolhouse Road, Pownal, VT 05261; phone: 800-441-5700. This book is tailored to the life of a busy mom. Step-by step instructions make this easy to use. Although the main focus is on freezing, drying and canning are also covered. I appreciated the section on preserving herbs. There is also a very helpful chapter entitled "What Went Wrong?"

BREAD

Secrets of the Masters Made Easy—Whole Wheat Bread Making by Diana Ballard, CFI Books, 925 N. Main, Springville, UT 84663, 1993. This versatile book covers bread made by hand, by bread mixer, and by bread machine. Common bread-making problems are explored, as well as all aspects of the bread-making process. Complete with directions for rolls, buns, bread sticks, pita bread, french bread, and more, this is a must have!

Uprisings—The Whole Grain Baker's Book by The

Cooperative Whole Grain Educational Association, The Book Publishing Company, P.O. Box 89, Summertown, TN 38483, 1990. This unique book is a collection of recipes from many small independent bakeries. It has some of the most interesting recipes, in addition to thorough directions at the beginning regarding how to use the ingredients. Illustrated directions for making different types of bread are very helpful.

MAGAZINES

Taste of Home, Reiman Publications, Customer Service, P.O. Box 991, Greendale, WI 53129; phone: 800-344-6913. *Taste of Home* is the combined effort of 1,000 country cooks across the nation. This bimonthly publication includes illustrated family-favorite recipes that are easy to make. Recipes do frequently contain meat, dairy, white flour, and fat. I often substitute healthier ingredients successfully.

The next two magazines have some philosophies you may find objectionable. Vegetarianism has associations with Eastern cultic religious philosophy. But if you can focus on a vegan diet for nutritional reasons, you will find here some great how-to information to help you cut down on or eliminate meat from your diet.

Vegetarian Times, P.O. Box 570, Oak Park, IL 60303; phone: 800-435-9610. I found this magazine to be full of detailed explanations about such things as how to plan a month of vegetarian meals. Short articles explaining how to use different vegetarian foods are especially helpful to those who are just learning how to integrate them more significantly into their diet.

Veggie Life, P.O. Box 412, Mt. Morris, IL 61054-8163; phone: 800-345-2785. This publication is very similar to *Vegetarian Times*. I recommend getting a sample issue of both to determine which you prefer.

Resources—
Chapter 4: Equipment

CATALOGS

Green Pastures—The New Resource Guide, Vital Food Sources, Inc., P.O. Box 1367, Flat Rock, NC 28731; phone: 800-295-3477. They carry Magic Mill grain mills, large bread mixers (I have both of these), and dehydrators. Water purification systems are also available.

The Urban Homemaker—**"Old-fashioned skills for contemporary people,"** P.O. Box 440967, Aurora, CO 80044; phone: 800-55-BREAD. This is one of my favorite catalogs for browsing to see what new equipment is available for homemakers. They carry K-Tec bread mixers and grain mills, as well as many other appliances. They also carry wheat and other supplies you may wish to purchase for bread making. An extensive listing of specialty books makes this a very useful catalog.

Ball Home Canning Catalog, Alltrista Corporation, P.O. Box 2005, Muncie, IN 47307-0005; phone: 800-240-3340. This catalog is illustrated and has everything you need to start canning except the canner itself.

Resources—
Chapter 5: Saving Money

Equipping the Family (*diaper service quality diapers*)
P.O. Box 3202
Glen Ellyn, IL 60138-3202
Phone: 630-588-0211.

Christian Financial Concepts, P.O. Box 2377, Gainesville, GA 30503; phone: 800-722-1976. Call for a free catalog. They publish a monthly magazine, *Money Matters*, offering encouragement to those seeking to manage their money according to biblical principles.

BOOKS

The Financial Planning Workbook by Larry Burkett, Chicago: Moody Press, 60610, 1990. This is the book that put our family on the road to successful budgeting. The worksheets are easy to use, and the book gives detailed instructions on how to set up and maintain your budget. This book could be life-changing for you.

Get a Grip on Your Money—A Young Adult Study in Financial Management by Larry Burkett, Colorado Springs: Focus on the Family Publishing, 1990. This is an excellent resource to teach your children sound biblical principles regarding their finances.

Debt-Free Living by Larry Burkett, Chicago: Moody Press, 1989. Unfortunately, many of us are saddled with debt beyond our ability to pay it off. In order to clean up the mess and start over, you need a resource such as this one to show you what to do. Highly recommended.

The Complete Financial Guide for Single Parents by Larry Burkett, Wheaton, IL: Victor Books, 1991. Whatever the reason behind your situation as a single parent, there are financial issues you will need to understand in order to be effective with your finances. Several chapters deal with the needs of widows.

The previous four books can be ordered through Christian Financial Concepts.

The Financially Confident Woman by Mary Hunt, Nashville: Broadman & Holman, 1996. As a former debt-ridden woman with more than $100,000 of credit card debt, the author now knows what it takes to handle money well. Her transparency about her own past financial problems gives credence to her suggestions, which she knows will work. Her straightforward style and down-to-earth tips make this interesting reading.

Saving Money Any Way You Can—How to Become a Frugal Family by Mike Yorkey, Ann Arbor, MI: Servant Publications, 1994. This well-researched, practical guide will give you specific information such as reviews of discount stores, frugality newsletters, and advice on coupons. Many resources listed in the appendices make this a good book to keep handy on the bookshelf.

The Tightwad Gazette by Amy Dacyczyn, New York: Villard Books, 1992. (Look for Volumes II and III also.) This mother of six has compiled many years of her frugal newsletter into three extraordinary volumes. It is easy to see that thrift is indeed practical as she shares hundreds of easy-to-implement ideas. Thoughts from readers are included, making this a great investment for those wishing to improve their methods. Buy the books since she is no longer publishing the newsletter.

A Woman's Place Is in the Mall and Other Lies by Karen O'Connor, Nashville: Thomas Nelson, 1995. Any woman who acknowledges she has a spending problem can benefit from reading this book. It is filled with hope for you as you read the author's story and those of others. Not only will you understand why you behave as you do, but you will receive help in changing that behavior.

1,001 Bright Ideas to Stretch Your Dollars by Cynthia Yates, Ann Arbor, MI: Servant Publications, 1995. These money-savers are inspiring and organized in a quick-to-read format. There is a testimony on the back cover from a woman with eighteen children who says she learned something new from this book after she thought she had learned it all.

A Woman's Guide to Financial Peace of Mind by Ron and Judy Blue, Colorado Springs: Focus on the Family Publishing, 1991. This book is written from the perspective of the different seasons in the life of a woman. Financial concerns are different in each season, yet each is treated with biblical wisdom. If your husband handles family finances, this book can help you be an encouragement to him.

Never Throw Out a Banana Again—and 364 Other Ways to Save Money at Home by Darcie Sanders and Martha M. Bullen,

New York: Crown Trade Paperbacks, 1995. Here is a quick-to-read book filled with easy-to-use tips. Many of these suggestions are the ideas you would have implemented had you only known about them. Well, now you do!

The Wholesale-by-Mail Catalog 1994 by Lowell Miller and Prudence McCullough, New York: Harper Collins, 1993. (I don't buy a new one each year even though they are available.) This book is updated regularly and includes hundreds of listings in a variety of categories. This is an easy way to save money as you find the best mail-order bargains to meet the needs of your family.

501 Sewing Hints, from the Sewing With Nancy series, Birmingham, AL: Oxmoor House, 1995. There is much money to be saved in sewing clothes for your family, but you need to know how to sew. This illustrated guide is quite helpful to the beginning seamstress who may be unsure of sewing terms or just how something should be put together. Those with experience will appreciate the shortcuts that are presented.

Choose to Reuse by Nikki and David Goldbeck, Woodstock, NY: Ceres Press, 1995. The concept of recycling and choosing to reuse is a definite money-saver. Although it is not written from a Christian perspective, the strength of this book lies in its endless resources for saving money. Many of their ideas should encourage you in the pursuit of a frugal lifestyle.

Resources—
Chapter 6: Holidays and Gift Giving

BOOKS

The Perfect Mix, 90 Gift Giving Ideas for Bread, Soup, Dessert, and Other Homemade Mixes by Diane Phillips, New York: Harvest Books, 1993. This book really got me excited last Christmas. Recipes for the mixes have gift tags with instructions for the mix that you just copy and attach to your gift. I was able to make up a lot of gifts in a short amount of time using this superior resource.

Scrap Saver's 101 Great Little Gifts by Sandra Lounsbury Foose, Birmingham, AL: Oxmoor House, 1994. This treasure contains full-color illustrations, full-sized patterns, and simple crafts that can be done quickly. Clear instructions are presented for seasonal as well as year-round gifts. Some crafts are suitable for children.

Make Gifts! by Kim Solga, Cincinnati: North Light Books, 1991. This is an illustrated collection of gift ideas for children to make. Many of the supplies are inexpensive and often items you already have in your home. Directions are clear, and my children find the projects easy to complete. You can probably find this at your library.

Other books by Kim Solga by the same publisher include: *Make Crafts!*, 1993 and *Make Clothes Fun!*, 1992.

Soap Recipes—Seventy Tried-and-True Ways to Make Modern Soap by Elaine C. White, Valley Hills Press, 1864 Ridgeland Road, Starkville, MS 39759; phone: 601-323-7100, 1995. Homemade soap makes a wonderful gift. This book contains complete instructions for the novice soap maker as well as new ideas for the old pros. The author worked together with professional chemists to develop mild soap recipes that were easy to make. Enjoy!

MAGAZINE

Crafting Traditions, Reiman Publications, Customer Service, P.O. Box 991, Greendale, WI 53129; phone: 800-344-6913. This colorful magazine has so many ideas that can be made quickly that I have found this to be a practical source of gift ideas. You may even wish to give a subscription as a gift!

Resources—
Chapter 7: Chores, Cleaning, and Laundry

PEGS™ *(Practical Encouragement and Guidance Systems)*
Family Tools, Inc.
P.O. Box 298
Circle Pines, MN 55014
Phone: 612-717-0644

After reviewing a number of organizational systems, I find this one to be the most versatile. The book that comes with the system thoroughly explains how to use it and provides parents with many useful ideas for ordering their family's day. This system has been very helpful as we develop a work ethic in our children.

BOOKS

401 Ways to Get Your Kids to Work at Home by Bonnie Runyan McCullough and Susan Walker Monson, New York: St. Martin's Press, 1981. This book is chockful of good ideas to get your family on track. I don't agree with everything they say, such as paying your child for certain jobs. Overlook what doesn't make sense to you and you'll have an excellent resource.

Clutter's Last Stand by Don Aslett, Cincinnati: Writer's Digest Books, 1984. There are many books written by this author to help you keep your home clean, but this is the place to start. Get rid of the clutter, and then you will be able to clean. The author's humorous writing style makes this a book that may be just the motivation you need to declutter.

Emilie's Creative Home Organizer by Emilie Barnes, Eugene, OR: Harvest House, 1995. I include this book here because if you want to keep your home clean, you need to get it organized. In addition to an entire chapter on cleaning, the author covers many areas of your home in a detailed manner. She has several other books on organizing that you may want to examine.

The Messies Manual—The Procrastinator's Guide to Good Housekeeping by Sandra Felton, Grand Rapids, MI: Fleming Revell, 1984. Although you may not like to see yourself as a "messie," there certainly are people who tend to be less organized than others. If you fit this description, this author can help you. A reformed "messie" herself, she knows what you are going through and has a plan that will help. This book is useful for everyone.

Messies Anonymous by Sandra Felton, 5025 S.W.114th Avenue, Miami, FL 33165; phone: 305-271-8404. This quarterly newsletter is designed to encourage you as you become more organized.

When You Live With a Messie by Sandra Felton, Grand Rapids, MI: Fleming Revell, 1994. Whether it is you, your spouse, or your children, living with a "messie" can be frustrating. Learn appropriate ways to influence your "messie" and how to create an environment that will encourage them to change. The author's humorous style make this great reading!

Clean and Green by Annie Berthold-Bond, Woodstock, NY: Ceres Press, 1994. In my efforts to provide my family with inexpensive, non-toxic household cleaners I have found this book immensely helpful. In addition to the many recipes for various cleaning applications, the author includes a listing of safe products and where they can be purchased. These are important considerations, particularly if you want your children to help with the cleaning.

Mary Ellen's Giant Book of Helpful Hints by Mary Ellen Pinkham, Avenel, NJ: Wings Books, 1994. This volume is a combination of three books: *Mary Ellen's Best of Helpful Hints*, *Mary Ellen's Best of Helpful Hints Book II*, and *Mary Ellen's Best of Helpful Kitchen Hints*. This book is filled with advice on how to get out of a jam—such as what to do if you get super-glue all over your hands. Many problems in our homes are easily solved if we just know how. The author covers her topic well.

Aunt Sally's Tried and True Household Hints, Avenel, NJ: Gramercy Books, 1993. Taken right out of Aunt Sally's journal, these old-fashioned tips are refreshing. She gets the job done without chemicals and commercial products. This would make a nice gift for a homemaker.

Resources—
Chapter 8: Organizing for Smooth Household Management

BOOKS

The Family Manager by Kathy Peel, Dallas: Word, 1996. This book applies successful managerial principles from the business world to the important role of homemaking. After clearly presenting her philosophy, the author gives practical instruction in time management, food management, managing home and property, financial management, special projects, family and friends, and personal management. She admits that she has a predominant right-brain orientation, which makes this a super book for those of you who may not prefer my left-brain-oriented methods.

Organizing for the Creative Person by Dorothy Lehmkuhl and Dolores Cotter Lamping, New York: Crown Trade Paperbacks, 1993. I found this book enlightening as I began to see why my husband organizes so differently than I do. If you feel that your right-brain tendencies are more developed than your left-brain tendencies, this is must reading for you.

Get More Done in Less Time by Donna Otto, Eugene, OR: Harvest House, 1995. Even the most organized person can learn new ways to streamline his or her life. This detailed presentation is encouraging reading as the author gives you a glimpse into her own life. I plan to go back and study this one.

A Mother's Time—A Realistic Approach to Time Management for Mothers by Elise Arndt, Wheaton, IL: Victor Books, 1987. As you are organizing your home to run smoothly, it is important to remember that you need to keep your time managed by priorities. This book will give you perspective as you try to implement new organizational strategies.

Confessions of an Organized Homemaker by Deniece Schofield, Cincinnati: Betterway Books, 1994. This mother of five children shares the how-tos of home management that have worked for her. Even though she knew what she should do, in the beginning she struggled to get it done. If this is your problem, her perspective may be the motivation you need to persevere.

PLANNERS FOR WOMEN

Linda Dillow's Classic Priority Planner—The All-in-One Organizer for the Busy Woman by Linda Dillow, Nashville: Thomas Nelson, 1977. This planner includes six Bible verses each week that will help you keep your priorities straight as you plan your week. Each week is nicely organized so you can see everything on two side-by-side pages. Priorities (Biblical), Things to Do, Weekly Schedule, Daily Schedule, Menu, and Shopping List are included. Separate sections accommodate annual goals, monthly plans (including birthday and anniversary reminders), and a place for phone numbers and addresses.

The Fruit of Her Hands by Diane Snyder, Colorado Springs: Focus on the Family Publishing, 1990. Containing many of the same features as the planner listed above, this one has a space each week for focusing on an area in your life that needs improvement. This is achieved through writing down daily action plans to produce the fruit you desire, receiving encouragement from God's Word, and writing down any fruit you have seen that week. There are pages in the back for listing books, sewing ideas, craft ideas, decorating ideas, gift ideas, and hospitality.

Resources—
Chapter 9: Home Business

How to Work with The One You Love and Live to Tell About It by Cameron and Donna Partow, Minneapolis: Bethany House, 1995. This is a thought-provoking exposé of what it really means to work at home as a couple. Transparent regarding their own strengths and weaknesses, the authors encourage workers at home in a practical way. Reflection and discussion questions at the end of each chapter allow you to use the book as a workbook to develop yourselves as successful entrepreneurs.

Homemade Business by Donna Partow, Colorado Springs: Focus on the Family Publishing, 1992. This book encourages women who are in the process of beginning to work out of their home. Questions at the end of each chapter stimulate appropriate actions to be taken at each point in the development and management of your home business. The only problem I have with this book is that it fails to adequately balance work and family, with the emphasis more strongly placed on work.

Working at Home, the Dream That's Becoming a Trend by Lindsey O'Connor, Eugene, OR: Harvest House, 1990. The author shares candidly about her own ups and downs as the mother of three small children and proprietor of her own home business. She systematically covers the process of working out of your home and helps you determine what your particular line of work should be. This book addresses the reality of taking on work at home and caring for your children at the same time.

Home Business Happiness by Cheri Fuller, Lancaster, PA: Starburst Publishers, 1996. A most encouraging book, this resource teaches how to do much of what is required for a home business in the context of sharing the real-life stories of successful entrepreneurs. This effective method covers such businesses as gift baskets, newsletters, desktop publishing, consulting service, and more. Many resources make this a very practical book.

The Selling from Home Sourcebook by Kathy Caputo, Cincinnati: Betterway Books, 1996. Many women are attracted to the flexibility and convenience of direct sales from their home. Beyond showing you how to set up your business and sell your product, this book lists detailed information about more than 120 direct sales companies. This is a big help to anyone considering home party plan type sales.

Homemade Money, How to Select, Start, Manage, Market, and Multiply the Profits of a Business at Home, 5th edition, by Barbara Brabec, Cincinnati: Betterway Books, 1994. Written by a woman considered to be a leading authority on home business, this comprehensive guide is the most practical book I have seen on the topic. It is loaded with advice on how to handle the many details of a home-based business. Since it is so easy to use as a reference, I find myself coming back to this book when I have a question.

Creative Cash—How to Sell Your Crafts, Needlework, Designs and Know-how, 5th edition, by Barbara Brabec, Barbara Brabec Productions, P.O. Box 2137, Naperville, IL 60567, 1996. This is the perfect resource for homemakers desiring to turn their craft hobby into a small business (or even a large one!). The author combines her extensive craft knowledge (she edited *Artisan Crafts* for five years) and business expertise in this detailed guide to help you in all areas of selling your craft. The extensive resource section makes this a book you will want to own.

Resources—
Chapter 10: Home Schooling

BOOKS

How to Homeschool—A Practical Approach by Gayle Graham, Common Sense Press, P.O. Box 1365, Melrose, FL 32666, 1992.

This is a great book to help you get started. Even after home schooling for several years, I am learning more each time I pick up this book. Easy to use, this book includes forms you can copy to help you get organized.

Educating the WholeHearted Child by Clay and Sally Clarkson, Whole Heart Ministries, P.O. Box 228, Walnut Springs, TX 76690, 1996. Here is a handbook for those of you who prefer to teach from good books and real life (this is our method). This teaching model is based on the wisdom of Charlotte Mason. If you want a practical approach to teaching your children without using conventional classroom methods, this is worth looking at.

The Home School Manual, 7th edition, edited by Ted Wade, Jr., Bridgman, MI: Gazelle Publications, 1995; phone: 616-465-4004. This is an incredible resource covering principles and practice from the early years through college. Special needs are addressed. This book is rich in home-school resources and even includes a section of record-keeping forms. Highly recommended.

The Right Choice—Home Schooling by Christopher J. Klicka, Gresham, OR: Noble Publishing Associates, 1992; phone: 800-225-5259. This book lays out the reasons to home school. Written by an attorney for the Home School Legal Defense Association, it is an in-depth answer to the many questions you may have about home schooling.

The Homeschooling Father by Michael Farris, published by Michael Farris, P.O. Box 479, Hamilton, VA 22068. This is a must-read book for every home-schooling dad. Beyond encouraging spiritual leadership in the home, the author gives practical suggestions for husbands to help their wives. Preparing your children for career, marriage, and citizenship are included too.

The Home Education Copy Book by Kathy von Duyke, published by Tim and Kathy von Duyke, P.O. Box 274, New London, PA 19360-0274. This is an exceptional collection of tips on getting and staying organized, complete with many forms to duplicate.

I like this book because I can design my own planner that meets the individual needs of my family.

The Home School Organizer by Gregg and Sono Harris, Noble Publishing Associates, P.O. Box 2250, Gresham, OR 97030; phone: 800-225-5259. This is a very detailed collection of forms to use to design your own organizational structure for your home school. Many of these forms spark enthusiasm for areas we may neglect—for example, hospitality.

MAGAZINES

Home School Digest, Wisdom's Gate, P.O. Box 125, Sawyer, MI 49125. This quarterly publication is a combination of articles from various authors on a variety of topics. I enjoy the depth of the articles and the thought-provoking nature of the content. Each article is only a few pages long, making it possible to read through the magazine in a series of short blocks of time. Advertising is all in the back, making it easy to quickly skim to see what is new.

The Teaching Home, P.O. Box 469069, Escondido, CA 92046-9069; phone: 800-395-7760, Subscriptions/Customer Service. This bimonthly magazine is filled with resources, encouraging articles, local state information, teaching ideas, and much more! My casual perusal of one issue informed me of an excellent unit study gardening package developed by a home-schooling family. It has been a great summer project that we would not have known about had I not looked in this magazine.

Notes

CHAPTER 1: LIFESTYLE SIMPLIFICATION

1. The Christian Homesteading Movement, Oxford, New York 13830, Mr. and Mrs. Richard Fahey and family.

2. Doris Janzen Longacre, *Living More with Less* (Scottdale, PA: Herald Press, 1980), p. 17.

3. Richard A. Swenson, M.D., *Margin, Restoring Emotional, Physical, Financial and Time Reserves to Overloaded Lives* (Colorado Springs: NavPress, 1992), p. 237.

4. Tim Kimmel, *Little House on The Freeway* (Sisters, OR: Multnomah Books, 1994), p. 75.

5. Larry Burkett, *Debt-Free Living—How to Get Out of Debt (and Stay Out)* (Chicago: Moody Press, 1989), p. 81.

6. Mike Yorkey, *Saving Money Any Way You Can* (Ann Arbor, MI: Servant Publications, 1994), p. 212.

7. "A Few Minutes for Mom," MOPs newsletter, Wheaton Bible Church, Wheaton, IL, April 1995.

8. Alvin Toffler, *Future Shock* (New York: Random House, 1970), p. 369.

CHAPTER 2: HEALTHY LIVING

1. Miriam Druist, *Heart Throbs of Motherhood—Meditations for Mothers*, Share-a-Care Publications, 240 Mohns Hills Road, Reinholder, PA 17569, 1992.

2. Baukje Doornenbal and Tjitske Lemstra, *Homemaking—A Bible Study for Women at Home* (Colorado Springs: NavPress, 1987).

3. *The Random House College Dictionary*, Revised Edition (New York: Random House, 1975), p. 433.

4. Ibid., p. 609.

5. Harvey and Marilyn Diamond, *Living Health* (New York: Warner Books, 1987), p. 124.

6. Ibid., p. 125.

7. Teresa Ann Dorian, *Eating Better Program Guide* (Salt Lake City: Nutriflex, 1993), p. 1.

8. Ibid., p. 2.

9. Betsy Carpenter, et al, "Is Your Water Safe?," *U.S. News and World Report*, July 29, 1991, p. 52.

10. Ibid.

11. "Fit to Drink?," *Consumer Reports*, January 1990, p. 31.

12. Ibid.

13. *Eating Better Program Guide*, p. 30.

14. Emilie Barnes and Sue Gregg, *The 15 Minute Meal Planner* (Eugene, OR: Harvest House, 1994), p. 320.

15. Ibid., p. 371.

16. *Eating Better Program Guide*, p. 9.

17. Harvey and Marilyn Diamond, *Fit For Life* (New York: Warner, 1985), p. 85.

CHAPTER 7: CHORES, CLEANING, AND LAUNDRY

1. *The Random House College Dictionary*, revised edition (New York: Random House, 1975), p. 238.

CHAPTER 8: ORGANIZING FOR SMOOTH HOUSEHOLD MANAGEMENT

1. Dorothy Lehmkuhl and Dolores Cotter Lamping, *Organizing for the Creative Person* (New York: Crown Trade Paperbacks, 1993), p. 20.

2. Ibid., front cover.

3. Sandra Felton, *The Messies Manual* (Grand Rapids, MI: Fleming Revell, 1984), back cover.

CHAPTER 10: HOME SCHOOLING

1. *The Random House College Dictionary*, Revised Edition (New York: Random House, 1975), p. 1348.

2. Ibid., p. 1393.

3. Ibid., p. 1511.

4. Ibid., p. 1247.

About the Author

Jackie Wellwood and her husband, Jim, live in suburban Chicago. They home school their six children. They also run a home business, Equipping the Family. They have made drastic lifestyle changes in order to lead a simpler life. They live in a modest-sized home, maintain a garden and many honeybee hives, and heat with a wood-burning stove. They work hard at reducing financial needs and protecting and promoting family values within a context of growing Christian faith.

What Others Say About
THE BUSY MOM'S GUIDE TO SIMPLE LIVING

"It blesses my heart to offer such a much needed book for women today. Simple yet simply complete."

—EMILIE BARNES,
AUTHOR OF *EMILIE'S CREATIVE HOME ORGANIZER*

"Longing for simple living? Jackie's guide will be a great help."

—ELISABETH ELLIOT,
BEST-SELLING AUTHOR

"A busy mom needs a simple lifestyle. Jackie makes 'simple' doable for a normal mom."

—CHERYL TOWNSLEY,
AUTHOR OF *FOOD SMART—EAT YOUR WAY TO BETTER HEALTH* AND *KID SMART! RAISING A HEALTHY CHILD*

"This book covers a wealth of practical ways to tackle the broad variety of home responsibilities from a biblical perspective. The section listing additional resources is invaluable."

—SUE GREGG,
AUTHOR OF *EATING BETTER COOKBOOKS*

"Jackie Wellwood's book *The Busy Mom's Guide to Simple Living* will bless those keepers at home who desire to nurture, to edify and to celebrate their families. It is a joy to reommend a book that explores the practical ways in which we can become excellent stewards of God's provision."

—TERRY DORIAN,
AUTHOR OF *HEALTH BEGINS IN HIM, BIBLICAL STEPS TO OPTIMAL HEALTH NUTRITION,* AND THE COOKBOOK, *HEALTH BEGINS IN HIM.*

DATE DUE

GAYLORD   PRINTED IN U.S.A.